Marrow of Light

poems of the heart's uncluttering

Brenda Peddigrew

poems 2016-2021

ISBN 978-1-7361332-6-2 (paperback)
ISBN 978-1-7361332-7-9 (digital)

Copyright © 2021 by Brenda Peddigrew

All rights reserved. No part of this publication may be reproduced, distributed, or transmitted in any form or by any means, including photocopying, recording, or other electronic or mechanical methods without the prior written permission of the publisher.

Printed in the United States of America

Dedication

I dedicate this book to all who have so enriched my deepening inner life, especially the Sisters of Mercy of Newfoundland, my colleagues and friends in other Congregations of women; my Aunt Bride (93 as I write this); Loretta Dower RSM, (92) who opened many doors of encouragement and affirmation for me over many decades; and especially AyunaJoan Weir, my daily companion for over twenty years, for her lively and positive encouragement, support, and practical wisdom in many different and still evolving forms.

Marrow of Light

poems of the heart's uncluttering

The stars this January night throb in place the way we on earth shimmer below our trouble…the shimmer throbs below the ache though (we) think it gone…Everyone I pass shows this shimmer…God, these stars tonight, I feel them mirror the galaxy inside where we dream of each other…(Mark Nepo in <u>Things That Join the Sea and Sky</u>, p.90

("how everything lives, shifting/from one bright vision to another, forever/ in these momentary pastures." (Mary Oliver, "Fall Song")

Look at it this way: There have been moments in your life when you had an experience that you know you will have to carry with you to your grave, because you are quite unable to find words with which to communicate the experience to anyone. As a matter of fact there are simply no words in any human language to communicate exactly what you experienced…You may try to communicate your experience in music or poetry or painting. But in your heart you know that no one will ever comprehend exactly what it was you saw and sensed. This is something you are quite powerless to express, much less teach, to another human being." (Anthony de Mello S.J. in <u>The Way to Love: The Last Meditations of Anthony de Mello</u>, p. 94).

The poems in **Marrow of Light** are my own attempt at communicating what cannot be truly described. These poems were given to me. I did not think about them or deliberately "make them up." My experience of "receiving" this poems was a bit like taking dictation…

Brenda Peddigrew
January 12, 2021

1. A Half-Second

The smallest breath of a breeze
turns everything, anything
into something else- a color,
a shape that wasn't there
a half-second ago.

No wonder it is said:
"The wind blows where it will;
we don't know where it came from,
or where it is going."*

So it is with our own lives
and the life of the world.

We never know. We never know.
A half-second can change
everything.

*John3:8

*****

2. A Path to Home

I know now, that I am too old
to walk the Camino
or go to New Zealand,
or even hike the high hills for very long…

I don't want to go anywhere.
But just now
I saw all my books laid out
like a stone path across a deep abyss
like a Giants' Causeway to the next life,
an illumination of grace
along which I could safely step.
A path to Home.

3. Against

Against all odds and logic
against mind's drivenness
against the urge to do more
get more, fill more, know more,
against all laws guiding my life
thus far -

I stand empty and waiting
content - it seems - to live
each moment, each day, as
it arrives, arms full of presents
Of presence. It is here, here
that Grail lives
and from here spreads
to the world. This is all
I know for now. In the
next moment
it could change. Or not.
My listening heart keeps
uninterrupted vigil, a cloistered
woman in perpetual silence.

4. Alive in Dying

This morning the trees are so alive in their dying
that I hear them calling to me, calling me over
like a friend, their leaves gesturing,
their branches swaying like belly dancers,
or like hammocks of invitation, hailing
winter's rest in stunning color that -
like all color - fades in its time.

But for the time that it's here - the colour of life,
the colour of love and friendship, the colour
of all the colours in the world - life itself
is a tapestry of color - and suddenly one day
you notice subtle shifts, barely
noticeable changes, a fading streak, perhaps,
or a blending never seen before. One day you notice
that what it took you an hour to do now takes three.
Some call this aging, this move towards transformation;
some call it dying. I prefer the latter.

What I am discovering is the hidden, subtle aliveness
in emptiness, in silence, in removing myself from
endless activity and social engagements.
Aliveness intensified; a spark billowing into a flame.
Life maximized in the falling away of unnecessary things,
showing itself in the simplest burning moments:
the trees' camaraderie; woodsmoke billowing among mists,
the loons' leaving cries, and the season's turning:
all there really is; all there is.

5. And Who?

And who will ease this lost
And despairing heart? Who
Will once again lead me
To the soul's water,
The Spirit's soul?

Who will wait just for me?
And offer comfort?
Not teaching or fixing or rescuing
But comfort with no conditions, no advice?

I am at the bottom of a deep well
Without water. Any turning
Brings me face to dark face
With black wet stone.
Only that.

Here I am. Here I am.

6. April Snow

Down it comes, an unexpected flurry
lasting all day. White and wet –
yet the ground doesn't change color.

Gray and brown, thirsty, thirsty
it drinks in every drop
of white wet snow
feeding its thirsty seeds
waiting to burst open with the next sun.

I am no different, no different.
I thirst
for the unexpected white
from an unknown sky
not to cover me, but to feed
and fertilize the seeds inside
waiting for water.

Anything can be white and wet.

7. Arms of Silence

Silence has approached me
and wants to be my friend – not
an obligatory friend –
not a must-do or should-do
but a friend of longing, a friend
of companionship.

She fills my body, resting finally
in my heart, leaving my body
tingling with alive joy.
Then I notice that she isn't
Only inside me – she is outside,
filling the world,
even the whole world. Noisy arisings
have no effect,
do not drive her away.

Only the noisiness inside me – ah!
thoughts, fears, angers, despairs –
stinging emotional pain –
these, these make me forget
her constant companionship,
her reassuring presence.

Yet these too have their place,
an inner ocean, rising and falling,
Often now
I recall them as reminders,
pushing me, pushing me
into the Arms of Silence.

8. Arriving

When I lived mostly mindbound
I didn't want to visit the graves
of my parents or my brothers –
I petulantly kept saying "they
are not there." Of course they are not.

But now, falling from mind
into heart, I long to visit those graves.
I long to stand, empty and silent
at the very place where they lie,
dissolved in the very earth
from whence they came, from which
I came and will soon go with them.

I long to be blessed again
by their earthly presence
and ask them, there in
their passing place
to prepare a place for me
and greet me when I arrive. For
I will not be leaving;
I will be arriving.

9. Ash Wednesday

Long ago, even knowing the glowing coal
that was my soul, holding it in my hand
without burning, I kept it hidden
in a pocket where it didn't burn through
but faded into gray ash. I didn't know
that the red fire stayed burning,
in disguise –

instead –

I leaped into the wondrous carnival of my mind
and stayed there, year after year
carried by the applause and the certainty
of doing good in the world:
I was told so. And I suppose I did.
Over and over I was told how I had helped.
And it carried me forward…

And then, late in life, the prop
of approval remaining, even continuing,
lost its nourishing fire.

It was only then that the glowing coal of my soul
diminished – now, as I thought – to a spark -
expanded as if breathed upon by a giant
and burst into flame. I stood
surrendering, as it became fire. I stand now
in its rhythm of tenderness
and grief, breathing in its expansion
and contraction – not my breath –

but Another mysterious Rhythm
blowing the bellows of my soul
and sending warmth to Mind,
who bows and thinks and speaks
relieved at her rightful place
in this beautifully unfathomable
Universe.

10. Attending

My spirit wants assurances
But my soul repeats a soothing "no" -
There are none to be given.

Oh - there are false ones - everywhere -
All around - all lasting about a minute, if that,
Some awhile longer, but not by much.

There are no assurances, really -
None but the small, constant flame
Burning within a sanctuary lamp
Of Being. Soul. Presence.

All else is passing.
All else is darkness.

All else but the small flame
Attending, steady, present.

11. Beech Leaves After Winter

I've only ever had my rejected self
though I tried all my life to live
into someone else's life for me –
and failed.

And here I am, becoming translucent
as a beech leaf in spring,
everything else worn away by ice and snow,
wind – yes, even wind – and still,
and still – the beech leaf clings
to the tree until new buds appear.

Then it falls to the ground, giving way
to the new. What admiration
I feel for beech leaves, dry and
papery, what stalwart bravery:
to fiercely cling – and to know
when to let go.

12. Core of Gold

Tomes have been written about silence,
inner and outer,
shallow and deep. Outer silence sought
is only a first step and even that
most people consider useless
at best or are afraid of at worst,
if they think of it at all,
which most don't. Not that silence
is anything to be afraid of:
it's what it reveals
that is the source of fear:
roiling inward unresolved angers
and fears, confusion
and lost loves.

But it's the inner silence that's the core of gold.
To suddenly burst through stone
into a soft cave of utter stillness
is
revelation.
Nothing, nothing going on outside you
can break its power,
unless you have lost your own power
in the silence that is your birthright,
the silence of the womb.

And are we not, even now, in a womb?
Are we not, even now
crowded and frantic, turning and seeking,
never satisfied,
never realizing that
there is an end to looking?

Isn't this the womb of choice
that we make with our frantic lives? And yet -
and yet - hidden in the inmost self is that core of gold.
It is hidden in silence. It is hidden in the letting go
of everything the world tells us is important,
and isn't.

The path opens only when a step
towards that inner cave
is taken, and all else,
all else necessary is given its place
and here you are, choosing that inner stillness
with abandon, risking and dipping and
opening only towards that cave,
letting go of everything else.

A door opens into blinding light.

13. Dark Dwelling

There is, after all, a light. Just as
eyes become slowly accustomed
to darkness
and begin to perceive shapes
and forms a thickness here,
a thinness there -

so with Darkness that is Soul -
resting in it, forms emerge, edges
and hints of shapes -

But only dwelling in darkness
invites them forth. Searching
frantically for light,
twisting away
from soft darkness
every which way one can
keeps me blind.

14. Disguises

Old veils are burning, burning away
from what they have been concealing…

What I thought was truth in time
only clothes a glowing energy
of being, of presence and
all the outer garments are now
in tatters, dissolving
in age and grace.

The veils were necessary disguises
for that bright essence, hiding it
from people I disliked or feared,
or thought strange and closed.
They protected the tender wounds
of pain, of hurt and loss, of misunderstanding
and excruciating self-doubt.

But now the veils are smouldering,
leaving holes the size of countries
or stars, revealing lights the size
of planets in every soul I know.

Age purifies the soul of all,
all its necessary disguises.

15. Dissolving:

So slowly it dissolves – the identity,
the trust that a life –
carefully, joyfully crafted
over decades –
will make the completion
easier, more secure, predictable,
peaceful.

Instead, a lifetime – dedicated, visionary –
dissolves. piece by piece,
capacity by capacity,
limitations, lost memory,
tear holes in that
once majestic garment

until it dissolves around your feet.

(for Marge Denis, 2018)

16. Emerging

After long years of searching for gold,
Inner and outer -
Peace, friendliness, helping roles,
Satisfying activities, creative expression
In word and image - love and grace -

I stop. Enough taking in.
What is actually there? What is there
When I stop taking in?
Who is there?

Beneath and behind all the roles, all the words,
All the searching and anguishing and wondering -
There is -
Nothing I can name. That nothing is everything.
That nothing is not even
the accumulation of a life search, but
a release of it. Only then,
Only then do I glimpse the essence that
Was always there, that would have been there
No matter what I did, no matter who I thought
I was becoming.

Hidden, pulsing, a spark of flame -
Essence...is this what is meant by
Those old words?
Mystery
Soul
Sin
Grace
Love -

I repeat the words like a mantra, calling forth
Their centuries of fire, their pulsing meaning
Still at the heart of all of life.

What is emerging is what everything has been all along:
Love. Just that.

17. Enough

Mind flows, an incoming tide
towards new books, new courses,
talks and teachers.
Then Heart says "enough.
I know all that is yours."

And the surging energy
like a tide
flows back
into the dark sea.

18. Eternal Emergence

Thick brown carpet of last year's leaves-
nourishing, nourishing –
raked away
reveal bright green shoots
leaping out of the ground
at my feet.

Circles upon circles upon circles
growing and dying
growing and dying.
Emergence
without end.

We live every moment
and all our days
in eternity.

19. MaCushla

Every morning I sit in dark silence
holding the world
warmed by wood's burning.
She is black and gold.
She is warm and tender.
She settles with sighs and purrs
While I rub ears and carve with love
her throat and back and tail.
She takes a deep breath and sleeps
beyond contented.

Would that there were
more such moments
weaving together our troubled world!

Would that moments of such contentment
spread their silence
a blanket of protection
a blanket of wrapped peace!

Perhaps then,
wars would die away,
no one having time for them,
and hatred become a story
in history books
and Love would be finally,
finally,
The Light of the World.

(February 8, 2017)

20. For Soul to Flame

What a fire needs is air.
All the good wood in the world,
carefully laid, dry – and of
different sizes – won't host flame
unless there is space between them,
allowing air to ignite and flame up.

Is it such a surprise then,
that the same is true for the human soul?
Crowded and busy, overworked
and overplayed – there is no room,
no breathing space for soul to flame,
to see deeper than skin and now,
to wait for the surprising arrival
of more than mind
(poor mind, thinking itself superior!)
waiting for more than mind can grasp?

21. For Uncle Vince: Reunion

This day last week you were out in your garage
getting your car ready for the winter. At least,
I imagine it so - that precious garage attached
to your house where you always were when we
went to visit, you working until the last minute, then
wiping your hands clean and taking off your
blue greasy coverall as you got ready to come
into the house for a cup of tea, already prepared
by Aunt Bernice. The two of you
were seldom apart, always ready for your eight
children and their spouses and your grandkids,
always ready for whenever and whatever they brought:
news, food, difficulties, illness, celebrations,
the need to move away, accidents and joys,
visits home.

When she died two years ago, you were bereft.
It didn't ease. You told me as much, the awful grinding
unending pain of it -
every time we spoke. At 86, you were determined
to stay in the big house, and did, continuing the
routines that wove you both together, inseparable
even in death. So when you went to bed on Monday night
you were no doubt noticing the empty side of the bed,
staying on your own side, wrapped in the emptiness.

Still, you slept. You didn't notice when the smoke started
its willowy way, feathery strands of white emerging
like a magician's trick through the walls. You didn't notice
when it tenderly reached your nostrils and throat, quietly
entering the last breaths of your good lungs, and softening,
softening your breathing until it stopped altogether. So then

you couldn't notice when the flames burst from the walls,
and quickly destroyed a lifetime of memories and
all the growing - of love, of children, of age, of memory, -
you couldn't notice. Thanks be to God for that.

We all loved you, Uncle Vince, last of my father's four brothers.
We loved your quiet presence, mostly talking only when
spoken to. And then - a story would burst out, into the conversation.
We loved your ability to dance, a skill my own father
never learned, and how you stayed so present to us all
into this 86th year.

You left us as you lived: quietly, suddenly, present in ways
we didn't always know - and yet - there you were. You left us
as you'd wished, and - without the fire's shock - we know
you are where you wish to be. All I see today is
Reunion.

22. Give Up

I must give up the burning longing
for steady connection
with another human being.

I must give up the expectation
of peace as a reward
for spiritual practice.

I must give up the hope of being good;
whatever I am is good, even when darkness claims me
completely.

I must give up judgment
and expectation of any kind: these are
the sparks of separation and suffering.

I am as I am and all is good.
All is good. All the dark descents
allow me to recognize the Light.

23. Gladly Giving Way

How readily the land offers up
what is no longer needed- offers
what has already given
nourishment
for what is new to emerge and grow

readily – let the old fall away

Let the new sprout, emerging
in its breathtaking green.

Let last year's growth
give way to the new.
Then – fall back, smiling.

24. Great Unfolding

Keeping heart-eyes on warm light
like sister-trees
like brother-birds-

everything falls away

and I am surrendered,
consenting with joy

to the Great Unfolding

(St. Bride's Littledale Chapel, 27 April, 2016

25. Grief

Something is broken in me
I cannot quite get the pieces
back together

Sometimes they slide together
just for a moment
but the slightest thing –
a change
an unexpected obstacle
a sudden hitch in plans –
and it will all come undone

It will come undone. And then tears
flood and flow.

26. Haiku

Shining indigo
Offers luminescent moon
Smiling night blessing!
(18 May, 2016)

Nothing else to learn-
Opening and deepening:
Gratitude and joy!
(6 June, 2016)

27. Hidden Beneath

Dry and faded, crackling
and shrunken – last year's leaves.

But a raking –removing the fully-given –
fresh tips of the new
laughing with energy.

Their time has arrived!

28. Home: When My Heart...

When my heart suddenly fluttered
coming down the five steps into the courtyard
after our morning walk
two days before Christmas -

I thought I was feeling an angel
opening her wings inside me, so great
was the unfolding, rising to my throat
and out my arms, taking my breath
and causing me to stumble.

Except I pay deliberate attention,
I am breathing shallowly
ever since. The angel
has settled her wings again, around my heart,
but I feel her readiness,
her vigilance, her waiting for the moment
when her wings must open again -
perhaps to claim me as her own,
and to fly me Home.

29. Supposing

I suppose it is
what am I doing anywhere?
This inner turmoil is not about
whether I am here
or there geographically or
in any particular physical space –

It is not about whether I am here
in my inmost soul, in
my inmost life –
no matter where I am.

That settles something.
Can't say quite what.

30. I Used To Know

There was a time I used to know - used to know everything
That I needed, and more besides. Most of it was helpful
To more people than myself, and they told me so.
I loved to ponder
How much good I contributed to the world, how
Satisfied - even justified - that made me feel.

Thinking about this now, I can't
Identify the moment it all changed.
I can't tell you the second or the minute -
Or the month or the day or even the year -
When everything blurred, when my soul
Shook me loose of such illusion, of such
Certainty and narrow seeing. I can't
Tell you -really -
How I fought with that blurring for years,
Cranky and resistant, thinking I was
controlling the uncontrollable.

And I can't tell you, really,
How once or twice the ground
opened at my feet like a yawn,
and I saw - oh rich boundless darkness -
I saw with inner eyes - the infinite universe
Living inside and outside, and how small I was
In it and how little I actually knew and would ever know,
And how knowing that expanded my heart
to the size of the universe and back again.

And how everything - everything - is unfolding only
As it can unfold. And how it must unfold, and how every
Moment holds the whole of time,
And every present moment is eternity.

31. I Want To

I want to now, I want to
give up all that I have learned,
all that I have gained
in all those years –

throwing it like seeds to the wind,
or the white blossoms presently
leaving the trees at wind's behest
and moment by moment by moment

being present
to the shining star of
NOW.

32. I Write

I write because
I have found my own life
in the words of others –
in their daring revelations
their trembling secrets
their shy and bold admissions.

May then my meager tentative efforts
shine a small flame in the darkness
for someone else –

Even for one person – this
would make all my efforts,
indeed, my life,
worthwhile.

33. Infinity

Sitting in this fraction
Of a moment, time
Disappears. Yet - instead
Of diving full out
Into the moment
I wait. This place
Of no time is unfamiliar,
Jolting.
Yet - nothing awaits.
(Perhaps everything awaits
But it no longer matters.)

Time stretches itself into infinity
Until I can't see it, can't even
Conceive of it, an endless
Thin line of light. I become
The light.

In this moment,
Questioning, uncomfortable,
Infinity lays a mantle
Over my shoulders.
I am claimed.

Lay down the pen.
Put away the book.

34. Into Focus

The bustling world is losing its grip
On me. Slowly, an unfamiliar
Focusing has begun -
Not chosen, not even known about
By me. Daily I am drawn,
magnetized into being,
Even though doing continues its necessity.

The grip of doing no longer matters.
Being is at its core, shining
And spreading. But who - who
Can understand this? Who
Can I tell?

None of these questions
Now holds any meaning at all.
When focusing finally falls into place,
Clarity stuns the eyes
And stuns the soul into silence.

35. Just As I Am

The white birch groves pull me
as strongly as the most powerful
magnet – like the family
I always longed for and never had –
welcoming, understanding.
holding me –
I lean into them and feel myself
embraced, embraced
just as I am
just as I am.

36. Let No One Say

Let no one say it is easy
to turn within and listen
to your own voice
lost for decades
or perhaps most of your life,
if ever heard at all.

Let No One Say that it's not work
to go against the tide
of wherever, however you live
to listen, to trust, to believe
that voice.

Everything in the world, except
the stalwart trees
and the earth's silence, which –
if you notice – surrounds everything –
everything – will push you away
from that patient, soft inner voice,
waiting for you. Just that.

But if you listen and believe, that voice,
that one alone
leads you home.

37. Life Strings

Thus are life-strings loosened:
Two younger brothers and cat companion
Leave the world, and
Daily companion wraps herself
mainly in her own life. Bereft.

Then- between and within a bursting second
Of time (whatever that is)
A yawning space
Opens
Not a beginning, not an end-

And a small turning orients me
Towards the Unknown -
Always there and just appearing.

38. Light of the World

Nothing I ever thought
would make me happy in life
ever did.
Too much striving. Never settling.

But the sight of new irises –
deepest purple –
among golden lilies, and the
sparkle of raindrops
on evergreen branches
and the air laden with spring incense:

these make everything else
a dull sham
while they glow with
the Light of the World!

39. Listening

I want to spend the rest of my life
listening. There is
so little of it in the world. Only trees,
warming in their roots now,
and plants, waiting for snow to melt,
and bears, emerging from hibernation,
and all wordless creatures
live their listening
flow from listening
follow only inner direction.

40. Living Life Backwards

"Not to worry," she* said-
"you are just living your life backwards-"

She didn't say it would end, or
how long it would take.
She didn't offer consolations or false hope
so common in our
frightened world.

No – only this –
I am "living life backwards"
and all the fear, resistance, denial,
pushback, anger,
despair, rage and deep loneliness –
all I refused to live
and blinded myself to –

now, now it rises like a tide
pulling me off my feet
and swirling me around, helpless
in an ocean with no land in sight,
nor even a small boat to carry me in.

I surrender. Is this then
true faith?

I know nothing. I am not the driver.
Inside though, as I write this,
something shifts…
a deeper surrender,
surprising trust.

*Sadhna Thakkar, N.D. – my trusted homeopath in California

41. to Catherine McAuley

It started that day in the house of your dreams_
in that room that was yours – full of grace, so it seems –
all your actual things – teacup and cross,
bedshirt and pre-dieu and all that was lost –
and for me –as if it a personal gift –
your writing desk, source of all that big shift.

I thought of the hundreds of letters it gave you
and how, even now, we all have them to stave off
the sorrows and suffering – a world of deep pain –
no stranger to you, though your letters would gain
a balance in face of it – joys you would share –
humor and laughter and projects to dare.

O Catherine, O Catherine – if you lived in our time,
I wonder if you would still write us in rhyme!
Somehow I think you would do even more
to keep all that darkness away from our door!
All the while praying and planning and dancing,
writing by email and joking and lancing
boils of our troubles and worries and woes –
but wait –
you are here, in the words at our doors.

Your letters, your letters – they brim with your soul,
and I feel all your shining; they make me more bold
to rejoice all through pain and to love without shame,
and how proud I am now to be graced with your name:
MERCY!

42. March

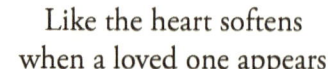

Like the heart softens
when a loved one appears

so snow melts when the March sun
breathes her softening breath

and trees call the sap
in their roots for winter
to rise,
to rise.

43. Light Still Comes...

(inspired by Louise Penney's "The Kingdom of the Blind")

Something new is forming. No shape, no hands
or eyes, no recognizable face or contour...
nothing familiar or attractive...and yet -
something new is forming.

In these Christmas days, filled for many
with shopping and parties and dinner
and drinking - filled with chaos, really -
the chaos of repetitive and mindless
expectation, of selfish spending and -
not realizing what is being
celebrated at all -

Light still comes into the world,
unaffected by anything we do, or destroy,
or lose or lament - Light still comes into the world -
even when any one of us is lost in the dark
for awhile or forever - Light still comes into the world.

Too soon yet. Too soon to see the shape
of what is emerging, what Light is making-
the Spirit that blows where it wills,
and no one knows where it comes from or
where it is going - that Light always, always,
coming into the world.

Looking for that Light opens faint pathways
in the dark.

44. Melding

Last night in the early dark
still with possibility –
two Barr'd Owls were singing
their mating calls. We stood
listening, gifts pouring over us
in streaming silence:
pure grace. Then –
looking up as stars appeared
one by one – the waning moon
was talking to Jupiter, so
close their haloes were melding.

What magic is this? This
moment filling the spring
night sky and two hearts
to breaking with wonder?

45. Mercying: The Real Work

(thanking Wendell Berry)

Just now, I sat on an uprooted tree
with spiders and ants for company,
wind gently stirring, making grasses
whisper.

I had no props, no activity, nothing
to justify my existence, nothing
I could point to and say :"Look!
I did that!" or even "we did that!"

A great heat of joy started in the soles of my feet
and rose, filling me
with peace. There is nothing I have to do,
even less, nothing I have to be –
except myself. The one, O God,
you gave me to be. The one who needs
no – repeat – no
justification by works. But Love – ah!
Love is a different matter.

You, O God, began me with love
and in it I must now continue.
When buildings are gone,
when institutions fail,
when plaques crumble, and even
memories fade –

Here you are, O God,
continuing the Love
that passed through me in my brief life,
continuing, continuing
the Mercying.

Let me know the love in which I was made.
Let me find it when I lose it,
for I have been trained to lose it.
And still it's there, twinkling and calling
me to go back to the beginning: to love
myself, to love myself with your love,
and to let all else
all else
all else
flow from that.

(Written for Mercy NL Chapter July 2017)

46. My Children

I thought I had no children
But just now realized that all
My unruly feelings
All my petulant complaints
All my bursts of impatience
And old, forgotten rage –

They are all my children
Just being born

So I can look on them with love
Hold and rock them
And offer them
For a transformation
I might never see.

47. Night Songs

1.

Somewhere out there in the dark forest
a coyote settles for the night
dreaming of hunting
at first light.

Somewhere out there the blue jays and the chickadees
have already settled in snowy branches
and trees sigh their passing into darkness
breathing their undetectable
nourishing warmth
into the cold March air,

while on the ground lights disappear,
giving ways to the constant faithful
lights of stars.

Don't tell me that animals don't feel,
can't love – my body's heart
knows otherwise. Or that seeds don't stir
stretching towards Light
far below snow, under ice
in the loose warm soil,
waiting their turn, waiting.

2.

Earlier in life I believed
teachers, lawgivers, priests, doctors –
authorities of every kind –
now I turn to my own pulsing heart
for truth – it rings there like bells –
of yes or no or time to let go –
of joy or warning.
My heart is tired of rhetoric,
or anyone who thinks they're right
and can save the world.
Of vested interests
of doing for its own sake
of religious righteousness,
rulers and corporations
including religious ones.

I have given up the shouting voices
for the whisperings of the Universe.

3.

This is not an easy passage, not
a joyful jumping from one reality to another,
not a fearless certainty. This
is a passage of sailing without an oar,
taken by unpredictable winds
in ragged sails, wondering
if the rudder
I thought was under the boat
is still there
or if it's been beaten off by shoals
or chewed by sharks or whales.

And yet the winds, the wind
that blows where it wills,
that mystery of arrival and departure,
that grace of unknown origin
and unknown destination –
that being carried and directed –
only that wind is trustworthy
only that wind
will bring me home.

48. No Moon Tonight

No moon tonight. I don't
go to lean against my tree –
I stand instead in the center
if the whole ring of trees

and feel their roots weaving a basket
to contain the darkness
within and without.

Invisible stars hover unseen
sending snow.

I stand in a world more real
than the lighted windows
of the house behind me.

49. No More

Endings don't take place
in long-planned
formal ceremonies.

Endings emerge – wisps of smoke –
companions to unplanned conversations,
realization forming itself afterwards:
no more.

No more will these people gather
in this way, for this purpose;
no more will I see these faces
or this particular light – no more
will it bring light to the world.

(St. Michael's Retreat House, Lumsden, SK, 1 June 2016)

50. Nothing Else

Sitting with tea in the 6am silence.
Not reading. Eyes Close. Heart
begins to warm, to vibrate. Feet
tingle - then warmth spreads -
flooding my whole body
flowing from my heart. Edge of sweating.

Thoughts, always milling, back away.
That's all. Alive.
Alive. Nothing else.

51. Nothing is Far Away

With the daily, hourly swirl of fright and threat and
War drums ringing through lines of light that began
As linking all people in friendship and benefit,
Energies of hatred, exclusion, and deliberate manipulation
escalate every day. Disturbance beyond imagination -
Echoed in erupting volcanoes, hurricanes, tornadoes:

All the earth is writhing in anguish and unpredictable
Disturbance. Even the polar ice cap is breaking and warming,
Sending animals and fish into despair and death, edging
Populations into movement unseen for centuries. War
and rumors of war, tensions now larger than
Biblical proportions and prophecies...and yet - and yet -

Here all around us is the silence of the forest.
Here all around us, spring flowers are emerging.
Here, all around us, summer crops are
springing from the earth and Bass fishermen
Begin their particular delight today.

I am grateful for earth and the waters of earth,
still soothing, refreshing and feeding us.
I am grateful for the coming together
Of summer people, the markets offering more
Than food and goods.
I am grateful for the rains, still able to nourish.
I am grateful for the dragonfly, the snake, and
Even the mosquito, fulfilling tasks
I have yet to understand.
I am grateful for the abundance that nothing
of the daily news yet disturbs.

Perhaps it helps - this small litany of gratitude -
Perhaps it helps to offset the anxiety, the fears,
The threats, the exaggerations, the deliberate lies,
The violence that deepens each day in the unfolding
Of our planet. Perhaps it is true -

That nothing is far away, and how we choose to hold
Each reality - all and not just one -
actually, actually - with others holding the same intention -
changes the world.
23 June, 2018

52. One Ordinary Friday Morning

Yesterday I visited an old professor
whose life had been given to poetry,
and now – decimated by Alzheimer's Disease –
the scourge of our rich, so-called developed world –
he sits alone in a fog of forgetting.
Except when lines of Irish poets –
Yeats, Kavanagh, Heaney –
are recited and his face lights up
and the lines finish themselves
from his mouth
from some place most think forgotten.

After that I went just down the road
to the land of a man my own age now –
seventy – who has created a sanctuary –
the word is not ill-used – a holy word –
for hurt, lost and rejected cats,
as well as deer, birds, wild turkeys
and bears, who visit his porch regularly.
I sweep and clean and feed the cats,
all the while listening to this intelligent,
large-hearted man,
whose softness compels him
to relieve suffering,
his real purpose in the world
though he is a precise and creative builder.

All this, in one ordinary Friday morning
before noon,
shines like bright light on the March snow:
I have to shade the eyes of my heart
from all the hidden goodness.

I have to allow my heart to expand
and glow with gratitude, breathing it in,
breathing it out.

There is so much more to the world
than I can see. There is so much more
than I can judge or understand,
caught as I so often am in my categories
and limited perceptions of how things are –
and worse and smaller-
how they should be. Instead,

the surprising light of what is hidden in the heart
when the mind is too busy
analysing,
evaluating,
categorizing,
deciding ---

that is the real treasure, the unspeakable joy,
and what sustains life when all the mind's
separations, evaluations, decisions
of what is good and what is bad –
all the mind's passing follies –
fall to the ground around that small
nearly unnoticeable shaft of light.

So whenever my mind demands – as it so often does –
"do something more important than talking to someone
who won't remember as soon as you go out the door",
or "what? cleaning up after cats and
coaxing them back into trusting people?" Whenever
that voice makes its appearance
as it often, often does –

I stop and remember John's eyes, reciting Yeats,
living every word in his confused mind
and crippled body. And I remember Don, lit
with joy as he speaks to his rejected cats,
and I consider myself given a heavenly gift.

30 April, 2018

53. Passing

There come times
when the longer deeper wider world
crowds out the passing
hurts and joys

and wraps me round

with soft expanding comforting
presence.

I live in both.

double realm*

*Brother David Steindl-Rast

54. Prayer

Sometimes a prayer
Passes through me
Like a shoot of heat,
A lightning bolt,
A beam of shade.

I greet it and send it on
To do its unknown work.

55. Presence

While tulip shoots rise from
frosted ground
subject to ice and snow still-

I rise and fall with weather and
behaviours of the wood stove
or the concerns of those
whose visions differ from
my own.

Standing beside trees, I am brought
to truest peace. Presence.

And all else swirls around
and away.

56. Questions

Younger, I was full of answers.
Older, I am full of questions.

Answers fell away when I wasn't looking.

Questions glow,
peacefully knowing
that the intensity
of their presence draws answers
like moth to flame!

But not
before the questions themselves
live for a long,
very long
time.

57. Reading Mary Oliver

When she died a few weeks ago,
I was as shocked as if a family member
had suddenly left for good. For days
I walked around, remembering
all the lines she'd written
about death, and the joy it brings,
the fulfillment of life, etc., etc.

Yet her leaving this
familiar world – of words, of trees,
of rivers, of all the animals
and especially birds she wrote about-
left me bereft, dark and grieving.

Now I am reading every word
she ever published. And here she is –
smiling and shining and pointing out
the world to me,
as she always has.

58. Release

Life is releasing me, letting go
of my desperate curious busy soul
transforming
transforming
it into Being –
only that –

an inner swelling
luminosity.

59. Sanctuary

Out in the world, I am
busy and engaged, overtalking,
overacting, buzzing like a bee.

Here, here is my desert in the ocean*
Here is my silence and rest, here
is my source of the eternal world
that does not pass away.

*David Adam's term "The Desert in the Ocean"

60. Dream

I once used to dream
of being lost in airports;
Now I dream of trees
And never think of being lost.

61. Just This. Just This.

a little cat was
sent to be my angel.
She is sweet and terrifying
fierce and tender - she belongs
to no one but herself.
Her green eyes flash and gaze.
She chews with sharp teeth
on my hands, then licks them,
as if apologizing.

She rolls over and begs me
to rub her soft throat
and furry belly. Then she turns over
presenting her back to be stroked,
sometimes endlessly.
She races all over the house
at a mad pace, up and down stairs
for exercise.

And then she settles in my arms
and nestles against my heart
and all is right
with her life and mine, in those
moments of soft presence,
warm communion.

My heart settles.

62. The Small Boat

Giving up reading, I discover
the deep moving ocean that
has been lapping its waves
inside me, more and more
insistent.
Since I learned to read
at three, and the small boat
that carries me, all adrift,
clearing the way
to landing in the next world.

Slowly, softly, tenderly
stroking MaCushla's belly
throat and ears slowly –
not in my usual rush,
not wanting to be done,
but feeling my whole being
in that soft, slow stroke –
that furry aliveness –

my inner world opens
like a flower formerly closed
and now, tenderly, tenderly –
a container holding (not only
the world)
but the Universe:
All One
All One.

63. The Turning of Stars

I.
In this frigid stillness
of an early January morning
my eyes opening first see
that bright morning star –
Venus –
opposite my window.
She blazes in the still-dark sky.
Her winter presence
stops me from rising
though the night wood would be
less than coals by now
And my waking mind blurry.

But Venus stops
my hurry to renew the fire,
to boil the kettle
to feed MaCushla.
She pins me to this moment,
reminding me
that the earth is turning, and
in a few weeks my waking
will not behold her:
she will be visible in another part
of the Universe altogether.

II.
Stars – all of them – move
and shift, always in a different place.
Venus – a week after I first notice her –
is already higher in the sky
than those few days ago.

And so are we. So are we.
Only – so caught up
in the outer world
my inner movement, subtle as Venus,
has also moved.
Notice, notice.

In this late afternoon
of my life, verging on evening,
Venus appears to me
like a vision.
But she is not a vision.
She is a beacon, as are all moving stars
in this magical universe.

64. Beyond That

Just now I built up the fire,
fed MaCushla, made tea,
sat here at the table
and stopped. Usually
I get right into reading
or checking Facebook.

But something stopped me
inside and out:
the early morning silence?
the expansion of the moment?

I feel it yet, as I am writing,
though these words
are emerging from
somewhere, somewhere…

"I am as full as an egg"
my grandmother used to say -
and that's how I feel,
though not in my body.
Full of something
that grows into something else –

My soul is burgeoning,
full of grace,
full of the dark unknown,
full of light.

Beyond that
I know nothing.

65. Emptiful

I see a place inside me now-
and it is growing, growing –
that empty and full all-at-once place-
from which I see
the shallow and passing nature
of everything, big and little,
in the large world,
and in my own small world.

This place appears to me
more and more frequently,
doing ordinary things
like watching the news, or
hearing yet again
the story repetitions
of family members, or of those
who struggle
and can't find a way through.

Perhaps all that is asked of me
is to hold them there
solutionless
and full of Presence.

66. A Glowing Coal

There are moments (and sometimes
longer than moments)
when Light fills everything –
the plants I am watering,
the washed clothes I am hanging on the line,
the stalwart trees in their daily vigilance,
one small flower, bending over –

And Light fills me in those moments
of mutual recognition –

a glowing coal of Mutual Knowing…

67. Aging Innocence

In aging innocence
I used to think
that if I did good things
people would see me
and that I was contributing good
to the world.

I would be recognized, accepted, affirmed.

Instead, in a sudden shift –
I am strong enough now to welcome
emerging truth:

Everyone sees only through the lens
of her own life – including me.

This truth is a kind of
skin-shedding:
both sorrow and relief.

68. No More

No more do I give in
to the haunting doubts.,
the repetitive questions
the inner scenes of self-doubt.

Instead I place a flame
right in the spot
where those voices appear
and the Light both stills
and replaces them.

69. A Million Tiny Attentions

After awhile - perhaps years – it's not
long talks that bond two people
but
a million tiny attentions.
No need of words –
but the million tiny attentions
bind and strengthen
invisible bonds
of souls –
never broken
never broken.

70. Disappearing

A small thread of smoke
appears suddenly in the air.
Softly
it thickens and pulls
all attention
to its being…until…
of itself
it thins and dissipates
disappearing.
So will I. So will we.

71. Whole Heart

My life is gushing up
like a tall fountain
filling me with joy and wonder.
No longer mine –
but given away
with both hands
and whole heart.

72. Silence

The more years I live through
the less I am sure of anything.
Life itself
so much greater than I knew
so much more
Incomprehensible.

Silence –
breathing, vibrant,
the Great Unfolding,
reveals Herself
the Source of all knowing,
and the Source
shining with increasing brilliance
until everything, Everything
is absorbed and illuminated
in its nourishing Light.

73. My Mother Knew

Once, after my Mother had been paralysed
a few years and was in hospital
for surgery to have the tops of
gangrenous toes removed,
I found her the night before
in tears, uncontrollably sobbing.

I got on the bed
and held her and asked
if she was afraid of the surgery,
or of dying.
She stopped, all at once:

"I'm not afraid of dying," she said;
"I'm afraid of life itself."

And now, older than my Mother was
when she uttered those profound words,
I realize the weights she carried
her whole life
and how privileged I was
to be there when she uttered
those words.

They explained everything.

74. Same Energy

The old drivenness,
building inner momentum,
has sneaked in under the door
like smoke,
like mist.

Once it was work.
Now it is tasks.

Same energy.
Stop.

75. Sparks of Prayer

Prayers rise like flames
from an empty heart
shooting to some unknown place
waiting to be heard.

Wordless, they disappear
like sparks
rising from an unknown fire
towards the Black Moon.

76. A Smoky Ghost

The habit of safety surrounds my soul
like armour, like a birthing sac,
like a horse's blinkers.

It arises now, a smoky ghost
on the dark edge of my awareness,
where it appears and disappears
at will – but not mine.

Not that I no longer need it,
but that it imprisons me,
keeps me from stepping forth
into a shining world.

77. A Slow Passage

a slow passage opens
and finally, finally
I begin
to arrive

into this world
the real world.

It is enough.

78. Exquisite...Light

underneath the skin:
Exquisite pain
pulses and pounds. Stripping
is underway.
Old resistances
habits
assumptions, certainties
preferences:
I don't yet know what remains.
I hope
it is Light.
I hope
to enter that stream
naked, stripped
inside and out.

(October 5, 2016, fourth anniversary of brother Keith's death)

79. Trace of Light

I am swimming through
a sea of illusions: momentarily
I see it, I see it.

And even so
my stroke is strong,
determined as I am
to finish my life
in calmer waters,

trusting, trusting the trace of light
that has guided me as long,
as long
as I have been alive.

(Thanksgiving Day, October 2016, sitting by the fire)

80. Soft

A softness has crept
into my certainties --- around me
everything unfolds.
A herd of cows I passed just now
will soon become meat
or give milk
inhabiting, nurturing
other bodies,
just as I too
will soon transform
into Light. Perhaps
I already am, without knowing,
like the cows.

81. Leaving the World

How will you leave the world?
Will you be like the black squirrel
lying on the road yesterday,
skin completely empty?
or
like the bird who flew too close
to a moving car,
her neck instantly breaking
and now still warm in my hand?
or
like the broken shell
of the snapping turtle,
still alive,
her dying stretched out?

Or the yearling bear, just finding his way
across the road,
struck by a mindless
truck-driver
who couldn't see the bear's majesty?

Whatever the pain
of leaving the world
I know this:
it leads to Light.
Like a sudden revelation, or
an opening in a dark sky
I see now
that it is the pain
of leaving the world
that brings more light
into the world.

82. Shifting the Wood

So often I notice
when the fire
seems to burn down
that
all it takes
is shifting the wood
out of its fixed position
to release the flames,
to flare up
in heat and light again.

83. Shards of Light

The dark forests with their
surprising shafts of light:
this is what claims me.

Not the brightness of the sun
nor the lit candles of thin trees –
but
these shards of Light
appearing
suddenly
unpredictably
on the dark forest floor.

84. Silence Waiting

Filling every moment
I miss what waits in Silence

Sliding into that place
where questions glow like gold
and answers fade
in their inadequacy

85. Another Energy

The sounds by which a fire begins
are almost negligible
if you are not listening
for them –
yet they are the beginning of
everything

there is another energy
just below the one
that lists what must be done
and drives me on to do it.

Just now I glimpsed it:
an emptiness, moving
like a vast quiet ocean
with no horizon

beneath all the things
to be done.

light after light
after light
falling into silence
relief
ah
unfolding.

Yet it all comes down to this:
throwing myself
on the slow roiling
of an inner tide

shifting and filling
longing for
sparks of light
waiting and waiting
and longing.

The world then
slowly appears
coming into clarity
out of a thick fog
I didn't know was there.

86. Nameless Poems

One day, if I am honored to die slowly,
to ease into dying-

I will know again these dark nights
full of stars –
these quiet hours
warmed with wood,
these privileged empty spaces
while the world spins
and cracks open.

I will not see what is born –
only feel the contractions
bringing it forth.

*****

87.

Tenderness isn't soft
but fierce –
rising up like flame
filling body
burning heart
searing eyes and hands
tending tiredness
and truth.
Burning

*****

88.

Everywhere, emptiness
darkness and disturbance
swirl like winter storms
blinding and choking
in the house and in the world.

Only the soft streaming of silent trees
standing in their regal presence
offer spacious solace _
and invitation
to fall into their arms:
just that.

What is this pain
that fills the night
and turns to tears
on waking?
that holds me
in its tight grip
and races through my being
with no abatement?
surrender
tears dissolving
loosening

*****

89.

Shifting into a different realm
swirl of stars in black skies
carrying my flesh and bone
tingling –
not with my life –
but with all life
all

the now
the once
the will be.

*****

90.

"I love being old" my friend said*
many times
during a short visit. And

I realized that I do too –
the long arc of experience
engaging with the world,
the knowing already
what younger people
will come to know,
the comfort
of being in the world

needing only soul as guide.

What grace! What gift! Knowing
that I love being old.
The night sky is familiar.

*(thanks to Candace Walton)

*****

91.

It was always God I was searching for –
that bright flame coming and going
in my child's prayers
refuge of my child's heart.

It was always God – not world, even
in the service of good.
Now, after a lifetime
of helping and serving
of fixing and rescuing –

I know –
my heart radiates with knowing _
that the bright flame
never left
never left
and it is all that matters. All
that matters.

Everything else falls away.
The Flame cares for all
I thought I did, or knew.

*****

92.

The world's turmoil rattles and roars
through every stability.
It has always been so.
It has always been so.

Without knowing
(I thought I had stepped out of it)
I am swept up and swung
into an inner tide
beyond my own making.

*****

93

Life as a relay race:
all beliefs, all experiences
only take you so far
and then there is another,
waiting
and on and on
into Brightness –
but there is no destination.

It is all here.
Now.

****

94.

Yesterday I stepped out of an old world.
Years, lifetimes
of climbing and searching
scrabbling over rocks and mountains
fending off blows
from equally frightened attackers

Falling blind and often deaf
that inner imperative
appearing long before

I was old enough to know
its name.

And its name is –
what this is –
is shedding. That's what
it comes down to –
over and over and over again.
Letting go.

A stepping, deliberately,
out of a dark struggle into
a light I sensed all these years,
a lifetime of years.

Now, with all unknown before me
I take another first step.

My own life, so terrifying
in its fullness –
I have tried to lose it

so many times
in the lives of others:
helping, rescuing, fixing, saving.

when only, only living
my one life
in truth, humility, love –
only that
only that
serves the world.

*****

My heart is growing. In battles where
mind and heart were in conflict,
mind always, always won.
Sometimes
I didn't even know
heart was present, struggling
for breathing space.

Now heart is primary and
it is not a comfortable choice.

Mind still shouts objections,
still struggles.
Balancing is delicate, necessarily
deliberate. Uncomfortable.

But no going back. No going back.

*****

95.

Every winter morning, wrapped
in a blanket of darkness
I put my hands into fire.
I build fire

I give air to fire
so it can better burn.
I burn.

This daily gift warms and steadies
an inner roiling
that refuses
refuses
to lie down in peace.

(Christmas Day, 2016)

*****

96.

The bottom falls out, if there
ever was one, or if
it was always
a false bottom.

Nothing is solid. Nothing
predictable, nothing
comforting

(except this warm kitten,
lying across my knees
seeking my hands)

emptiness. darkness
no consolation.

Thus the year ends.
Thus the year begins.

*****

97.

I am in the winter of my life.
No matter
how many earth seasons
come and go

before my good body
is claimed by the
Mother of All –
no matter –

Silence and snow
rest and receptivity
fill my soul…

while the roots of my life
draw down and inward
the rich lifeblood
of all my years.

Grace and Peace!
Love and Blessing!

*****

2017

98.

I feast on seeds of words
rising unsought,
unbidden,
in my dark soul.

I listen. I write. I return.

The seeds blossom.

*****

99.

MaCushla in these early mornings
pulls me into silence. I cannot
read or write while she is in my arms,
nose tucked into my elbow
purring with joy
lying on my lap
leaning into my arm
front paws tucked under at the first joint.

All reading and writing flee, flee
while I rub soft ears,
golden throat,
thickening black fur
and gaze into steady aqua-green eyes,
opening and closing.

Such absolute presence, such silence,
such shimmering heart in this moment!
such gift I could never dream of!
All desires, needs, plans dissolve
in this passing moment
of pure presence: MaCushla.

*****

100.

All my life
I have found my worth
in taking onto my own shoulders
into my own heart

the emotional burdens of others.
all the while

longing for someone

not to need me
but to see me.

*****

101.

Where once I knew – ask me almost anything –
I could talk about it, advise a choice,
sure and certain I knew, explaining,
explaining –

Now I know nothing and the emptiness
holding all my words
allows for no explaining.
There is none adequate, or close to true –
a child's babble,
rightfully rejected.

While the world surges and swirls
in empty words and I swim
in stillness, wordless
wonder…

In all things I thought to do
failure reigns:
welcome!

*****

102.

A great weight greets me
every morning now
sitting where my stomach
used to eagerly anticipate
breakfast

It gathers during the night
eating my dreams
getting full.

Then it sits inside all day. I carry
it around as I would a cat,
or a small child.
Sometimes, briefly, I forget it,
but only briefly.

Then words emerge.
I used to think
the weight impeded the words.
but now I realize
it is giving birth to them.

*****

103.

I have myself.

*****

104.

When I go down,
when I dare to dive deeper
than any part of my life
has ever before claimed –

I lose the gift in getting there –
in glimpsing that achievement
and feeling satisfied.

I lose the gold –
that short glimpse-
a flash, really,
of that vast emptiness,
waiting to receive,
waiting to receive.

*****

105. Some Questions

+What do I need to throw like a stone
in the river, never needing to know
if the current takes it
or if it sinks to the bottom?

+ What do I need to lift from my heart
lightening the load it was taught
to carry all those years ago?

+ What will fill the space when I release
what I am carrying? How will I know? How
will I not just fill it again?

+ How can I allow the snow-laden trees
to shake me into their stillness,
into their silence?

+When will I invite in the Emptiness
that has stood at the door
of my overflowing house for
most of my life, offering
only peace and joy,
which I could not receive?

*****

106. Edges

There are edges clearly visible
inside me, sharp as blades. They
appear suddenly
in the breath between moments,

seeming
as if someone provoked them
but they are no one else's doing.
They are my own edges
unsmoothed by years of denying
hiding and covering – and
God help me –
stepping over them-
as if they didn't exist.
But they insisted
and now appear before I know it.

They are my edges.
And they did their work –
they saved me. They protected me
and even –
and I can't forget this –
they nourished me.

But now – now
they need no embrace
but my own. Just mine.
I thank my edges
for all they have done. And

with blessing, with blessing,
with love, with prayer,
I give them back.
I send them into the Dark Mystery
from which they came.

*****

107. Contentment

Every morning I sit in dark silence
holding the world,
warmed by wood's softly
burning flame.
She is black and gold.
She is warm and tender.
She settles with sighs and purrs
while I rub ears and throat and back.
Then she sleeps, deeply breathing,
contented.

Would that there were more such moments
weaving together our troubled world.

Would that moments of such contentment
spread their silence
a protective blanket
wrapping peace.

Perhaps then
wars would die away,
no one having time for them,
and hatred become a story
in history books,
and Love would finally be
The Light of the World.

*****

108. Deer Sister

Every morning and late evening
I walk through
a madhouse of thoughts,
an asylum of feelings
to a door called "Love".

Sometimes I can open that door;
sometimes voices
claim me
before I can turn the knob.
But I always return. And when
the door opens

I step into the Beautiful Silence
a profound Emptiness
a presence always
waiting to receive
a rich Nothing
from whom
the whole world – day after day –
comes forth.

Less and less can I be part
of the non-stop world
of over-filled time.

Less and less can I speak words
that hold so many meanings,
so many experiences

that shared meaning can't get near
the exchange.

Presence is lost
in the pressure of more to do,
Lost
in the hurried time-bound momentum,
a skiff skimming surface waves.

Doing barges on.
a freight train at high speed.
No time
for deepening. No time
for Being or – God forbid –
Being Together.

*****

109. Get Up

Last night the Worm Moon
was a disc dominating
the sky, silvery and brilliant,
spilling light
far over its edges, a waterfall
in all directions.

And below, its breezes
surging through old snow
reach the worms
sleeping beneath frozen earth,
stirring them, stirring them.
"Get up" the Worm Moon says,
so they move in restless blindness
opening the way for sprouts
already beginning
the journey upward.

And I, standing out in the dark frozen air
lit only by the Worm Moon
and the stars
that penetrate its brilliance –

I feel the same stirring in me,
that restless sprouting
of new shoots, that
mushing and moving together,
that wormy grace.

*****

110. Longing

I gathered my longing
like a basket to my chest
and it burst into flame,
spreading outward
towards all the known
and unknown
world around me.

Arms crossed, I held the fire
for all
who need a spark of hope
to take the next step
into their lives.
I don't need to know.

I only need to keep the fire going.

*****

111. April Snow

Down it comes,
an unexpected flurry
lasting all day. White and wet –
yet the ground doesn't change.

Gray and brown,
thirsty, thirsty,
it drinks every drop
of wet white snow
feeding its thirsty seeds
waiting to burst open
with the next sun.

I am no different. I thirst
for the unexpected white
from an unknown sky
not to cover me, but to feed
and fertilize the seeds inside
waiting for water.

Anything can be white and wet.

*****

112. Pain

Today's pain
is one long needlepoint
filling my whole body.
I try to
love it, hear its message
which I cannot decipher.
I try to hold and rock it
like a baby. Tears
run through me
a river of springs
but I can hardly breathe
with the presence of it,
filling
my whole being.
Pain of helplessness and loss,
pain of frustration and silence
pain of love and anger –

*****

113. Opening Arms

If you lean into
the wall of pain
you will eventually
fall through
into peace.

If you run or push away
from the wall of pain
It will pursue you
and close in
no matter
what you try
what you try –

except opening your arms
and holding it close
in an embrace of tears.

Then the world opens.
The tears complete
a wholeness.

*****

114. The Whole Breath

The day is coming
and is not far off-
I see its horizon –
when I won't be able
to do much –
mostly just
be in the world,
breathing "here"
until breathing stops
and breath returns
to the Whole Breath
of the pulsing Universe.

I might as well practice now
inhabiting that silent space
of being, of oneing with trees
and birds and all the
silences
that truly create the world.

My own silence
leaps out joyfully
at this invitation.
My own silence
blossoms like a late flower
unexpectedly
swiftly
fully
knowing nothing
wanting nothing.

*****

115. This Came To Me

Am I tired yet
of being a conduit
for words
my mind
never thought up?

I thought I was
but now – perhaps not –
perhaps the words have
just piled up
behind my closed door
and are gently knocking
"let us out, let us out."

So I will. And will see.

*****

116. Visit More Often

Visiting myself
early one morning
as I often do, over tea,
I notice – and not
for the first time –
an inner racing,
an urgency to get going,
and even to stay going,
which translates
into doing.

This is not pleasant company.

"I must visit you more often"
I overhear myself saying,
"why don't we just sit here awhile,
resting?"

I notice a shrivelled response –
resistance, in might be called –
and a tiny tiny heartshift
of relief.

All my life I've been
doing and going,
moving and pleasing,
contributing and helping.
Not that there is anything
wrong with that,
but it's just not
the whole story.

"The Whole Story" must include
that tiny shred of self
who survived all these years
waiting –
and here is her turn –

not only to be seen
but to be pleased,
just in her being.
Just in her being.
The rest she doesn't want or need.
For her gifts bloom
like flowers in her being,
rising joyously,
a fountain of heat
and light.

*****

117. Birth Pain

When words are missing.
may they return
from wherever
they have been wandering,
thinking they were lost
but really –
gathering more light.

When pain takes over the world
may I know that it is only
the pain of birth.
and will give way
to the next explosion
of everlasting life.

When I cannot see through
prevailing darkness,
may I know
blinding black
as the womb
of next Light.

*****

118. That Light

Every day inspiring words
are given to me. It is
not enough. Words from outside –
though they stir energy,
a swirl of recognition –
are not enough.
Not enough.

No – it is the swirl itself
the nameless stirring
the present light
that calls and calls.

Every time I turn
to that Light
it is there.
It is there.
All else falls away.

*****

119. Soul Home

"Go home", says the voice inside,
almost shouting
in the ear of my heart.

I know this is not referring
to the Rock where I was born, though
that is tempting – but only briefly.

No, this Home is the home
of my deepest soul. It has
called me all my life, and
waited, waited. Now –
time is getting short for me
to bring her into the world,
to live from her,
to flow each day
from her insights and knowing
without apologizing to the world.

Though it is morning, darkness
prevails. Looking out,
the solar lights still illumine
the path to the door.
Where are my inner solar lights,
the ones that reveal the path
leading to my Soul?

*****

120. Enfolded

Stepping into the house
silence wraps around me
a soft blanket.

I am enfolded.
My skin welcomes and warms.

*****

121. Here, Now, Alone

Now that the boats have stopped
for the night, ducks and gulls
are returning to their bobbing
nd gliding on the water. Meanwhile
the baby eagle sits vigilantly
on his branch, surveying the ground,
and just now, I met a young skunk
in the labyrinth, who paid
no attention to me whatsoever.

In this moment the world is at peace,
everything in its place.
Here, now, alone – this moment –

and in the next moment
anything could happen –
ah! the pink sky.
the pale blue water
the pulsing silence:

this is what goes on. This is what
goes on.
(Loretto Maryholme, 2017)

*****

122. Home Light

In this slow descent
of the downside of the arc
called aging, when the body
sighs and the soul soars,
a Great Light appears far off
and it is Home. Slowly

all else orients towards
that Light, that
Compass of the Heart.

Finally, finally

I am down to my own words –
the ones written in Light
inside my soul, emerging
out of nothing
and becoming
Everything.

*****

123. Hidden Canal

There once was a doorway
I could have slipped through –
and didn't.

Now – now I glimpse that stretch-
that holding of opposites
in tension –
that paradox-

as opening me to a larger world,
one I couldn't have had
making one choice.

And life is larger, wider,
richer, for all the smaller choices
carrying me, unperceptively,
slowly,
along that Hidden Canal.

**(written in Searson's Pub on Baggot Street, Dublin,
just down from the Canal near Mercy International Centre
Mercy Day, 2017.)**

*****

124. In This Moment

Finally, nothing outward matters,
so changeable is its nature,
so constantly
transforming and passing.
I just glimpsed

that permanent Light, even as wind
blew leaves and pine needles
preparing for rain.

(poems found here and there)

Questions for the Between

So here it is - done! Thirty years (and really, 72)
passing like poured water,
arriving now at a place so unfamiliar
that settling contains only a few seconds
of clear sky at a time. "You exaggerate"
you might say - but not a shred -

What is it, I wonder now, that allowed
so much to be done, and so easily?
And what is it now that wrinkles time
so deeply that all those same things
appear at once, and impossible in the moment?

And even further: when will it settle?
And what does it take to invite it to settle,
then allow it to do so?
And what if it doesn't settle at all?

So here is the moment of faith -
Real faith, I might add -believing
that the rise and fall, the swirl and stream,
the race and rowing, the rhythm of
the light and dark, the swirling seasons,
the sickness and dying, the small gains
and larger losses - on it goes, on it all goes -

And the trust that standing still,
opening within, receiving now,
more than giving - it is all one ribbon
of the streaming colors weaving
in and through the river that is life!

Table Roses

The darkening roses, still in
their petal shapes
tell the heart of this story:
it's what we thought was true,
eternal, evolving – that is dissolving:
the face of the world.

Interdependance of countries
turns out to be a weakening, after all,
as we all fall like dominoes,
one chasing the other, falling
on the next, and all – all
for one reason:

unlimited greed, forgetting the Mother,
Earth: our first and necessary Home.
The darkening roses in a vase
on the table in front of me
tell the story.
(23 April, 2020)

Except Mary Oliver

In these early mornings
silent with the magnificence of All
I am reading less and listening more.
One by one, books
have disappeared from my
morning pile – except
Mary Oliver – whose poems
have swung around me
and through me, over and over
these many years and continue
like the perennial seasons,
each time
becoming clearer in grace,
in presence, reminding me
again, again, again
"to let the soft animal of my body
love what it loves" and that
"when we die the body breaks open
like a river;
the old body goes on, climbing the hill."
Do I need any more words than these?
Does anyone?

Still, there are times I forget myself
and go searching in books
for what I already know,
for what Mary Oliver told me
decades ago.

Every year, every faithful year,
the trees make beautiful buds,
tender and true
in their particular forms.
Then they drop them to the soft earth,
trusting their future.

Going Down in Glory

This year I am spending more time
watching the great gold
releasing itself, leaf by leaf,
one by one, sometimes
highlighted in the red glow
of another floating companion.

This year I am more steeped
in awe at this vision than
all the previous autumns
of my seventy-two years,
especially breathless at the free golden carpet
we are being given
on the floor of the forest,
hiding the deep green moss,
deeper than any carpet
in the richest mansion.

And this astounding vision
raises the question: how am I
changing with the seasons of my own life?
How am I
offering to the world
all the gold of transformations I have
known and witnessed?
Certainly not as richly coloured,
or as freely abandoned as these leaves,
filling my eyes
every day.
Certainly - not yet at least –
as surrendered as they are.

Every day now, I spend time
under the trees, asking guidance,
Receiving their wisdom,
moving as they move, surrendering
to the wind alone.
Every night, I go out again,
receiving the moon's light, the stars'
wheeling through the heavens,
and the river's endless flowing -
like the leaves, going down in glory.

The time ahead of me
is not endless.
Spending it with leaves
and stars and moon and
flowing river is balm, is the welcome
of arms opening
to a soft floating
back into universal Light
and Grace and Peace.

*****

The Door of Silence

Every morning, Mary Oliver
would go outside and sit
with her notebook, listening.
She wasn't listening to the birds,
or the wind in the trees,
or the soft silk of running water,
though they often
speak in her poems - no -

she was waiting
for an inner voice to speak -
she was, she says herself,
taking dictation.

Lately I am shocked to realize -
that's how my own poems
arrive. Words
run through me
onto a page, into a poem,
and best in a dark early morning
when stillness
opens the door of silence.

In this way, every day,
I too feel that
opening the door of silence –
inner silence, I might add –
though it is helped by
outer emptiness of sound -
every day
more and more words
slide through

that door, though sometimes
it is only a crack,
not a door fully opened.
I am not sure I could
stand the door fully opened...
but perhaps that
is being saved
for my final step –
that wide emergence
into blinding light,
where words pour and pour,
wrapping me in a cloak of welcome,
and I no longer need to write them.

*****

A Weaving of Trees

All I want now
is to sit surrounded by
thick forest silence
wrapped in a weaving of trees.

Everything else that I am compelled to do
removes me from this: the blanket
that thickens in silent air;
the wrapped Presence, Nameless

Yet I can't stay in it long. I can't
sit still enough. The last joy
of my life will be to open,
release, receive, and
be carried home.

*****

Awaiting Nothing

A settling silence surrounds me
within and without this dark morning.
The day's light hasn't yet arrived -
yet in me, after years - after a long life
of inner struggle -
a sudden peace -
a grace of surrender-
is given. However brief...

and I know it as gift.
I know it as not mine to make happen.
I know it as grace -
and mine only to accept,
not control, bring about or imprison.

Here I am, sitting in the early morning
darkness and silence
awaiting nothing.

*****

Nothing Asked of Me

This morning there is nothing
but the rain,
pounding and pouring,
thunder punctuating
her urgent sentences.

Wood heat fills the house, making
a cave of dark warmth. Nothing -
nothing else exists for these minutes
of silence, sitting alone
at the kitchen table, a strange
settling peace before the day begins.

My heart expands: no pressures
today. No appointments. Nothing
asked of me for now. Instead,
I pour my prayers onto my brother,
stranded in Frankfurt, and onto Joan
driving to Bancroft - and to all those
unknown and in need of something
only prayer, only ever prayer,
can bring.

Only now, deeper and deeper,
do I glimpse
the impersonal brutality
of the world:
meaningless, random,
and the outpouring of love,
equally present.

*****

The Dark Unknown

I.

Lying face down in the pit of desolation
Darkness. Hopelessness. Perhaps this is
true surrender. I give up
trying to make anything else happen.
Everything just is what it is.

But what it is...

It doesn't work
to look on the bright side.
It doesn't work
to manipulate people and events
so I can feel better.
It doesn't work
to "put my mind somewhere else."
These tricks all feel false,
manipulative, controlling.

No - surrender is the only inner prayer
that feels - ironically -
solid and true.
I don't know anything, anything -
except the sinking,
the utter aloneness,
the release of all, of my own life,
into the Dark Unknowable.

II.

Skin stripped away - blood, veins, bones
exposed. Exquisite,

particular pain,
numbing the mind,
pounding the heart.
Waiting - in the knowledge
that all attempts
to escape are transient,
futile. Another
Light is burning me through,
purifying
something. All I can do
is surrender and wait.

As long as it takes.
As long as it takes.

And meanwhile,
meanwhile be tender
and compassionate to all the world.

I have tried other ways. They don't work.
And are false, false and empty.

Only the burning away illumines soul

*****

All the While

I have lived too long
on the surface of things, while -

all the while -
the Great Empty Fullness
held me in place, waiting,
and not always patiently -

No, now - when Doing is nearly Done,
I sink back, gingerly, tentatively,
surrendering to what I do not know
and letting go
of all I thought I knew.

Longing, I open my arms and some
unfamiliar contentment rushes in, even if only
for a few seconds.
It is enough to take me through the day.
It is enough

*****

Only That

Sitting here, inner world erupts
sending outer world into disarray:
staying here in the inner world -
faithfully, constantly, forgivingly -
all with struggle -
holding the formless, cradling it
like an infant, while it twists
and kicks and stretches
in all directions - that,
only that, is now my calling
for as long as I inhabit this world
and long, perhaps forever,
into the next.

Everything, everyone, is bright
with emptiness –
nothing to clasp
or hold
in solid connection. As soon
as a word is spoken, a gift shared,
an insight flashed –
it is gone. It is
gone. That space surrounding
everything, everything;
inhabiting
the seen and the unseen,
melding
the world - only that.
Only that.

*****

A Shiver of Tears

The world is watered by tears.
I can only believe
that they make things grow -
dissolve the old, soften
hard ground, water inner seeds,
call forth new life where death
appears to be the ruler.

Every day more tears appear,
especially if one watches
the daily news of wars, deaths,
floods, murders, and all the ways
humans dissolve the world-
bringing tears - to soften,
to dissolve.

Is it tears then,
that water the world
into to life?
Are tears the great dissolvers,
the powerful softeners
for what is next
meant to emerge?

As my own body feels
a shiver of tears running
through it almost every day,
feels the softening they bring,
the readying for new light,
the dissolving of tight darkness-

Let it be so. Let it be so.

*****

Eldering Opens the Door

1. One Lit Leaf

Gazing through
the tasks of the day ahead,
eyes unfocused, heart-heavy, I
looked up from my tea - and saw -
one lit leaf, framed
in a small square of the glass door
leading to the screened porch.
Many leaves were visible,
surrounding
it in dull green, almost dark.

But only one was lit by a stray ray
of the new sun. It burned
into my eyes
entered me
made the day possible.

One lit leaf opened the door
to the day.

2. *Releasing Time*

Now begins the loosening.
No more
deadlines,
must-do-now's, absolutes.
Inner space opens up:
a great swirl
of indeterminate possibility

knocking me off
ego's self-definitions.

Here, in the thick and comforting silence
before the day swings into action,
I sit full with emptiness
held by an elusive Presence
longing to stay
in this still, undemanding moment:
Time released, releasing me,
releasing itself.

3. Settling

The silence this morning is so still
so thick, so present, wrapping me
like a blanket - so comforting;
it won't even allow me to read.

"Hush, hush," it breathes, "stay still -
I am holding you.
Everything is done
that you were asked to do
and more.
Relax, relax in my arms."

Tears rise. Body softens.
Silence moves closer - into mind,
into heart. "All is
as it is meant to be"
she whispers.

4. Window Cleaning

Just now, listening within,
I remembered the windows -

all the windows in this
many-windowed house,
which I
vowed to clean, one by one,
this summer.

And then I laughed out loud!
It's my inner windows
that need cleaning,
that are begging to be cleaned!
Begging me to find a cloth
that will remove the years
of too many words
of too many books
and thoughts
and repetitious meanderings!
And too many worries
and over-caring and
unrealistic responsibilities
and self-inflations!
All needing -
wanting asking begging - to be
wiped clean.

Now I know-
window cleaning
the real kind, the harder kind,
is the primary work
of this summer.

5. *Time Opens Up*

I never before realized
in my careful planning
narrowed
by self-satisfaction

that with every plan,
every
commitment to
every community-
I was shutting time's window.
Nothing else
even occurred to me about that
committed block of time.
It was placed and closed in the
calendar of commitments.

It never occurred to me, never
until now, that time could become
in that way, so fixed -
so limited. Now
the opening of time
suddenly yawns before me
in dawn colours, and the impulse
to fill it falls away
falls away, like water
from the sides of a boat,
a small boat, surging oarless
through a great sea.

*****

Anything Else

All I want – or ever wanted – is for someone
to see me. See me in a way I would know
myself seen. Recognized, accepted, loved; unquestioned,
as in "what do you mean by…?

No advice. No teachings that would lead
anywhere else, any better place, or
better understanding of the world. I am
done with all that, having spent
all my lengthening life searching for
such guidance, such recognition.

Instead, my warming heart radiates
as I write this, echoing a ring of truth,
sounding like a great chime in a high tower.
There is nothing else now –
except the mixed light of my whole life,
moving like the Aurora Borealis
in the darkening sky.

Is this (finally) love?
I cannot see it
as anything else.

Jutting Stone

The fullness of loss and its isolation
surrounds me like armour
and lives inside me, a starless
moonless night. I see myself
sitting on the thinnest end,
almost a point,
of a jutting stone stretched out
over a dark valley
whose walls are barely visible
so far away they seem.

I cannot see bottom at all
over which my stone hangs,
and I wonder whether it will crack off
and release me into
bottomless darkness at some
unexpected moment.
Every morning I am here
and sometimes during the day.

Being Stilled

Slowly, slowly, plane by plane
car by car, the world
becomes still. Ordinary
activities, unrushed, fill
the day.
Nothing –even last week –
could have prepared us –
any and all of us in this world-
for this sudden choiceless stop.

We are being stilled.
We are being transformed.
We are receiving
what we could not –
wandering wild and frenzied
in the world – bring about
ourselves, for ourselves.

Really, is anything as startling,
stopping or sobering
than this?

Our healing taken
out of our hands,
plans disrupted,
money lost,
shockingly, shockingly
we are not in charge.

And a settling – if
we allow it so –
if we recognize the gift –
begins.

Table Roses

The darkening roses, still in
their petal shapes
tell the heart of this story:
it's what we thought was true,
eternal, evolving – that is dissolving:
the face of the world.

Interdependance of countries
turns out to be a weakening, after all,
as we all fall like dominoes,
one chasing the other, falling
on the next, and all – all
for one reason:

unlimited greed, forgetting the Mother,
Earth: our first and necessary Home.
The darkening roses in a vase
on the table in front of me
tell the story.
(23 April, 2020)

Found: Infant Grace

All my life, I have been on a search -
Hidden even from myself - or perhaps
It was a pilgrimage - for someone, anyone,
Who would mirror the understanding
I never had, never had, never fully knowing
What I was searching for or why -

Though a line of people genuinely loved me,
I know that - but without the understanding
I sought. And I - not really knowing what I sought -
Until now.

A small ripple of understanding, of love
Has finally opened a chasm into
Some streaming light, an understanding
only I can know, only I can give myself.
I turn
And peer into that streaming light
And open my arms and heart
To the infant waiting these seventy two years.

*****

Golden Light

Finding its way through the thick leaves
of this abundant summer,
Sunlight this morning is pure gold,
shining all it touches, however briefly.
On this table where I write, Sunflowers stare at me -
exaggerated gold,
laughing with joyful abandon.

Switching attention, Golden Light
pries open my shaded heart,
and - for a few seconds -
heart not only beats but
vibrates with Light, and sends
a wide smile through every cell of
my warming body. Even soles of my feet
tingle and burn.

Golden Light, I glimpse now,
is a gift always there, seen or unseen.,
felt or unfelt. It takes a slight shift,
the slightest turning of attention -
and there it is.

Wherever We Land

Yellow leaves are beginning to slide,
gracefully, from their trees,
Floating, floating - they don't know where -
but throwing themselves
onto a path of unknown destination.
They are beautiful in their trust,
in their surrender
to what is larger than themselves.

My eyes follow them. I feel a sharp pull
to float with them
and to trust where we land, trust
that it's just this surrender and landing
that transforms the world
and prepares the soil for new
and unspeakable growth.

All my life I weighed the wisdom
of what I would say: inner warning bells
were installed earlier than speech.

Now my own truth (mostly) overrides
such pondering. And I trust now
that how it might be received
is not the primary consideration
but only, only the truth itself -
like the yellow leaves, falling
and floating wherever the breeze takes them,
and content with wherever they land.

*****

Going Down in Glory

This year I am spending more time
watching the great gold
releasing itself, leaf by leaf,
one by one, sometimes
highlighted in the red glow
of another floating companion.

This year I am more steeped
in awe at this vision than
all the previous autumns
of my seventy-two years,
especially breathless at the free golden carpet
we are being given
on the floor of the forest,
hiding the deep green moss,
deeper than any carpet
in the richest mansion.

And this astounding vision
raises the question: how am I
changing with the seasons of my own life?
How am I
offering to the world
all the gold of transformations I have
known and witnessed?
Certainly not as richly coloured,
or as freely abandoned as these leaves,
filling my eyes
every day.
Certainly - not yet at least –
as surrendered as they are.

Every day now, I spend time
under the trees, asking guidance,
Receiving their wisdom,
moving as they move, surrendering
to the wind alone.
Every night, I go out again,
receiving the moon's light, the stars'
wheeling through the heavens,
and the river's endless flowing -
like the leaves, going down in glory.

The time ahead of me
is not endless.
Spending it with leaves
and stars and moon and
flowing river is balm, is the welcome
of arms opening
to a soft floating
back into universal Light
and Grace and Peace.

*****

The Door of Silence

Every morning, Mary Oliver
would go outside and sit
with her notebook, listening.
She wasn't listening to the birds,
or the wind in the trees,
or the soft silk of running water,
though they often
speak in her poems - no -

she was waiting
for an inner voice to speak -
she was, she says herself,
taking dictation.

Lately I am shocked to realize -
that's how my own poems
arrive. Words
run through me
onto a page, into a poem,
and best in a dark early morning
when stillness
opens the door of silence.

In this way, every day,
I too feel that
opening the door of silence –
inner silence, I might add –
though it is helped by
outer emptiness of sound -
every day
more and more words
slide through

that door, though sometimes
it is only a crack,
not a door fully opened.
I am not sure I could
stand the door fully opened...
but perhaps that
is being saved
for my final step –
that wide emergence
into blinding light,
where words pour and pour,
wrapping me in a cloak of welcome,
and I no longer need to write them.

*****

A Weaving of Trees

All I want now
is to sit surrounded by
thick forest silence
wrapped in a weaving of trees.

Everything else that I am compelled to do
removes me from this: the blanket
that thickens in silent air;
the wrapped Presence, Nameless

Yet I can't stay in it long. I can't
sit still enough. The last joy
of my life will be to open,
release, receive, and
be carried home.

*****

Awaiting Nothing

A settling silence surrounds me
within and without this dark morning.
The day's light hasn't yet arrived -
yet in me, after years - after a long life
of inner struggle -
a sudden peace -
a grace of surrender-
is given. However brief...

and I know it as gift.
I know it as not mine to make happen.
I know it as grace -
and mine only to accept,
not control, bring about or imprison.

Here I am, sitting in the early morning
darkness and silence
awaiting nothing.

*****

Nothing Asked of Me

This morning there is nothing
but the rain,
pounding and pouring,
thunder punctuating
her urgent sentences.

Wood heat fills the house, making
a cave of dark warmth. Nothing -
nothing else exists for these minutes
of silence, sitting alone
at the kitchen table, a strange
settling peace before the day begins.

My heart expands: no pressures
today. No appointments. Nothing
asked of me for now. Instead,
I pour my prayers onto my brother,
stranded in Frankfurt, and onto Joan
driving to Bancroft - and to all those
unknown and in need of something
only prayer, only ever prayer,
can bring.

Only now, deeper and deeper,
do I glimpse
the impersonal brutality
of the world:
meaningless, random,
and the outpouring of love,
equally present.

*****

The Dark Unknown

I.
Lying face down in the pit of desolation
Darkness. Hopelessness. Perhaps this is
true surrender. I give up
trying to make anything else happen.
Everything just is what it is.

But what it is...

It doesn't work
to look on the bright side.
It doesn't work
to manipulate people and events
so I can feel better.
It doesn't work
to "put my mind somewhere else."
These tricks all feel false,
manipulative, controlling.

No - surrender is the only inner prayer
that feels - ironically -
solid and true.
I don't know anything, anything -
except the sinking,
the utter aloneness,
the release of all, of my own life,
into the Dark Unknowable.

II.

Skin stripped away - blood, veins, bones
exposed. Exquisite,
particular pain,
numbing the mind,
pounding the heart.
Waiting - in the knowledge
that all attempts
to escape are transient,
futile. Another
Light is burning me through,
purifying
something. All I can do
is surrender and wait.

As long as it takes.
As long as it takes.

And meanwhile,
meanwhile be tender
and compassionate to all the world.

I have tried other ways. They don't work.
And are false, false and empty.

Only the burning away illumines soul

*****

All the While

I have lived too long
on the surface of things, while -

all the while -
the Great Empty Fullness
held me in place, waiting,
and not always patiently -

No, now - when Doing is nearly Done,
I sink back, gingerly, tentatively,
surrendering to what I do not know
and letting go
of all I thought I knew.

Longing, I open my arms and some
unfamiliar contentment rushes in, even if only
for a few seconds.
It is enough to take me through the day.
It is enough

*****

Only That

Sitting here, inner world erupts
sending outer world into disarray:
staying here in the inner world -
faithfully, constantly, forgivingly -
all with struggle -
holding the formless, cradling it
like an infant, while it twists
and kicks and stretches
in all directions - that,
only that, is now my calling
for as long as I inhabit this world
and long, perhaps forever,
into the next.

Everything, everyone, is bright
with emptiness –
nothing to clasp
or hold
in solid connection. As soon
as a word is spoken, a gift shared,
an insight flashed –
it is gone. It is
gone. That space surrounding
everything, everything;
inhabiting
the seen and the unseen,
melding
the world - only that.
Only that.

*****

A Shiver of Tears

The world is watered by tears.
I can only believe
that they make things grow -
dissolve the old, soften
hard ground, water inner seeds,
call forth new life where death
appears to be the ruler.

Every day more tears appear,
especially if one watches
the daily news of wars, deaths,
floods, murders, and all the ways
humans dissolve the world-
bringing tears - to soften,
to dissolve.

Is it tears then,
that water the world
into to life?
Are tears the great dissolvers,
the powerful softeners
for what is next
meant to emerge?

As my own body feels
a shiver of tears running
through it almost every day,
feels the softening they bring,
the readying for new light,
the dissolving of tight darkness-

Let it be so. Let it be so.

*****

Eldering Opens the Door

1. One Lit Leaf

Gazing through
the tasks of the day ahead,
eyes unfocused, heart-heavy, I
looked up from my tea - and saw -
one lit leaf, framed
in a small square of the glass door
leading to the screened porch.
Many leaves were visible,
surrounding
it in dull green, almost dark.

But only one was lit by a stray ray
of the new sun. It burned
into my eyes
entered me
made the day possible.

One lit leaf opened the door
to the day.

2. Releasing Time

Now begins the loosening.
No more
deadlines,
must-do-now's, absolutes.
Inner space opens up:
a great swirl

of indeterminate possibility
knocking me off
ego's self-definitions.

Here, in the thick and comforting silence
before the day swings into action,
I sit full with emptiness
held by an elusive Presence
longing to stay
in this still, undemanding moment:
Time released, releasing me,
releasing itself.

3. Settling

The silence this morning is so still
so thick, so present, wrapping me
like a blanket - so comforting;
it won't even allow me to read.

"Hush, hush," it breathes, "stay still -
I am holding you.
Everything is done
that you were asked to do
and more.
Relax, relax in my arms."

Tears rise. Body softens.
Silence moves closer - into mind,
into heart. "All is
as it is meant to be"
she whispers.

4. Window Cleaning

Just now, listening within,
I remembered the windows -
all the windows in this
many-windowed house,
which I
vowed to clean, one by one,
this summer.

And then I laughed out loud!
It's my inner windows
that need cleaning,
that are begging to be cleaned!
Begging me to find a cloth
that will remove the years
of too many words
of too many books
and thoughts
and repetitious meanderings!
And too many worries
and over-caring and
unrealistic responsibilities
and self-inflations!
All needing -
wanting asking begging - to be
wiped clean.

Now I know-
window cleaning
the real kind, the harder kind,
is the primary work
of this summer.

5. Time Opens Up

I never before realized
in my careful planning
narrowed
by self-satisfaction
that with every plan,
every
commitment to
every community-
I was shutting time's window.
Nothing else
even occurred to me about that
committed block of time.
It was placed and closed in the
calendar of commitments.

It never occurred to me, never
until now, that time could become
in that way, so fixed -
so limited. Now
the opening of time
suddenly yawns before me
in dawn colours, and the impulse
to fill it falls away
falls away, like water
from the sides of a boat,
a small boat, surging oarless
through a great sea.

*****

Anything Else

All I want – or ever wanted – is for someone
to see me. See me in a way I would know
myself seen. Recognized, accepted, loved; unquestioned,
as in "what do you mean by…?

No advice. No teachings that would lead
anywhere else, any better place, or
better understanding of the world. I am
done with all that, having spent
all my lengthening life searching for
such guidance, such recognition.

Instead, my warming heart radiates
as I write this, echoing a ring of truth,
sounding like a great chime in a high tower.
There is nothing else now –
except the mixed light of my whole life,
moving like the Aurora Borealis
in the darkening sky.

Is this (finally) love?
I cannot see it
as anything else.

Jutting Stone

The fullness of loss and its isolation
surrounds me like armor
and lives inside me, a starless
moonless night. I see myself
sitting on the thinnest end,
almost a point,
of a jutting stone stretched out
over a dark valley
whose walls are barely visible
so far away they seem.

I cannot see bottom at all
over which my stone hangs,
and I wonder whether it will crack off
and release me into
bottomless darkness at some
unexpected moment.
Every morning I am here
and sometimes during the day.

*****

Being Stilled

Slowly, slowly, plane by plane
car by car, the world
becomes still. Ordinary
activities, unrushed, fill
the day.
Nothing –even last week –
could have prepared us –
any and all of us in this world-
for this sudden choiceless stop.

We are being stilled.
We are being transformed.
We are receiving
what we could not –
wandering wild and frenzied
in the world – bring about
ourselves, for ourselves.

Really, is anything as startling,
stopping or sobering
than this?

Our healing taken
out of our hands,
plans disrupted,
money lost,
shockingly, shockingly
we are not in charge.

And a settling – if
we allow it so –
if we recognize the gift –
begins.

*****

? Questions for the Between?

So here it is - done! Thirty years (and really, 72)
passing like poured water,
arriving now at a place so unfamiliar
that settling contains only a few seconds
of clear sky at a time. "You exaggerate"
you might say - but not a shred -

What is it, I wonder now, that allowed
so much to be done, and so easily?
And what is it now that wrinkles time
so deeply that all those same things
appear at once, and impossible in the moment?

And even further: when will it settle?
And what does it take to invite it to settle,
then allow it to do so?
And what if it doesn't settle at all?

So here is the moment of faith -
Real faith, I might add - believing
that the rise and fall, the swirl and stream,
the race and rowing, the rhythm of
the light and dark, the swirling seasons,
the sickness and dying, the small gains
and larger losses - on it goes, on it all goes -

And the trust that standing still,
opening within, receiving now,
more than giving - it is all one ribbon
of the streaming colors weaving
in and through the river that is life!

*****

Seeing the World

I.

Without my knowing it, the trees
turned me into one of their own -
a rooted walking presence-

My quaking soul stands with them
and always has. Not knowing it
didn't matter. They knew.
Held and grounded,
my roots moved with me, connecting
me to them in deepest earth,
connecting me
to the pulsing silence
of the smallest forest.
Now coming into life's late afternoon,
I feel their gathering around me again,
like lit candles, waiting and still,
swirling the air around me with love,
preparing me for transformation.

II.

So many say "I want to see the world"
and to most that means travel -
but I would say now "me too" -
I want to see
that Blue Jay who just came to the feeder -

I want to see the pine needles
in their obedient line
on every twig;
I want to hum with the river
in winter flow,
singing in its constant voice.
I want to hold my breath
at the tracks of deer and rabbit,
fox, wolf and turkey - even fisher -

and at the night sky, bright with moon
rich in stars, or completely, utterly
dark with magnificence.

This is the world I want to see.
Sometimes I wonder if it
lives inside me, and not just
outside.

*****

Only Here

It is only here - this solitude,
this empty heart - everyone else
gathered around but not in
my innerheart - that I know
who I am. Finally, if briefly.

And that those to whom I feel closest
are inside my inmost heart:
they do not feel tears rush through my body;
they do not feel my darkness;
empty of everything, however brief;
they do not feel the silence filling me;
they do not notice the forgotten flower,
half hidden in a ditch, waving;
they do not see the worms in the road,
or the frog crushed by a passing car;
(and if they did they would probably not remove them)
they do not feel that rush of blood, that helplessness -

I could go on. But why? Everyone,
Everyone feels her own heart alone,
and it is only Love, and Love alone,
in all its winding forms
that opens any Heart, and only for a breath -
any longer would be unbearable -

to see and hold and be the world!

*****

The Poem Beneath the Poem

The poem beneath the poem
slowly emerges into words - before,
it was a negligible tide
a shifting, ever so slight,
easily ignored - but now,

now the tide has become a wave,
and the wave is rolling and growing
in size and swing -
who knows when it will become
a rogue wave? Who knows
what the tide will bring in,
flooded by its shifting waters?

We will not be ready. Every day
we will shift, even an inch, toward
the unknown. Some days it will be
several inches, or a foot, or a mile.

Who knows if we will ever reach
a steady place again?
And what does it matter?

Life will carry us...Earth will carry us,
The smallest plants and sweeps
of rain and snow will carry us, insects
and rabbits and deer and fox will carry us,
rivers and the great ancestors of trees
will carry us - and if we will not
be carried now, then we are lost.
Until Earth finds us again.

What is breaking down
is really breaking open.
What is ending
is really transforming.
We live in a time
of both/and, not
either/or.

Stand steady. Stay
in the Heart, not the mind.

Trust
the Illumined Darkness

The Magnificent Whole

For that split second only - looking
at the trees outside the screened porch
from my early morning place at the kitchen table-

the raindrops on them sparkled -
sparkled! in all possible colours -
and in a few seconds, went back
to being indistinguishable raindrops
on a leaf's dripping edge.

Isn't this the way we all - everything
created -(which is everything) -
live in this world?
We sparkle awhile, perhaps even
a few times - and then we are
restored to our natural inclusion
with the whole of created life,
blessedly indistinguishable
from the unfathomable glory
of the magnificent Whole.

*****

Stream of Grace

Rain, pouring and pelting,
Keeps us in, containing us,
delaying the morning walk,
offering instead this delicious - yes -
delicious silence. Only the rain,
that soft gift, can be heard.
Now and then a birdsong
as they shelter in the trees.

This is my morning heaven.
This is my stream of grace.
This is the day's beginning,
the world remaking itself,
after resting in fertile darkness,
steeped in silence.

And isnt that how we too
are remade?
Steeping in the silence of sleep,
and the silence of the dark and
fertile emptiness
of the world?

*****

Tide

I.

This morning there are only tears.
I cannot read the usual inspiring words in books,
though I brought them to the table.
There are only wordless tears
rising and falling inside me, - a tide –
and all I need to do is lie down on the tide
and be held, be blessed, be moved…
Be. (not do)
The tide will shift and turn in its time
And I with it.
But there is only the Tide.

II.

Wind is blowing but I cannot hear it.
I see only the soft waving of the flags
and hear the gently chiming of the garden bells.

Now, nothing. Wind
is taking a break. Blue –
bluer than blue
is the cloudless sky.

Why isn't that enough?
Why aren't I – just myself –
enough?

*****

Settling

When words arise unbidden
I know myself to be
in my true and unending home.

And though they are
announcing themselves
they are surrounded by
the Great Darkness,
rendering them small
but not helpless, not unimportant.

Every word coming from that Home
arrives on wings, floats like feathers,
settles in the dark crevices of the Heart,
and propels through time and space,
fuel for Life's unbidden journey.

Listen. Receive. Stop Searching.
Receive what is always, always
being offered
in the dark depths of
Soul.

****

Shedding Like Feathers

All my props are
falling away. I was
such a good girl!
Dependable, steady -
knowledge was always,
always my armour
until now.

The armour is melting.
My familiar shape dissolving.
The edges of my form
are blurry, fuzzy.
Somewhere in the melting mess
a pinprick of light
appears and disappears.

She has been living on her own,
waiting. Now she is coming forth
more often, and sometimes
growing
in size and intensity.

I have no idea
where she is going
or who she means to be -
only

everything that once
defined her/me
is shedding itself like feathers
and nothing is yet
emerging,
no form is taking her/my place.

Who is this silent inward light,
this sanctuary lamp
burning while holding quiet,
dissolving the old need
(or ability)
to speak?

Who is this, content
with the wordless Light
of Love Alone?

Who?

Who is the one who is stopping?
Who is the one who is sinking,
while another gently waits
to come forth?
She has been waiting all my life,
holding, tending, shifting
showing herself in moments only,
in flashes and then –
stepping back, stepping back,
waiting.
Is her moment here?

Cruising the Downside of the Arc

Frequently now,
I see my own life
as an arc.

Birth, growth and increase,
being part
of an ever changing community,
colourful and shifting and
moving through
Breathless gains and
heart-stopping losses...
And arc after arc,
crossing one another,
Intersecting and dissecting
the energy of the world.
energy of all
strands of life moving
through an ordinary day.

Only now, as I begin
to descend the downside
of that arc, do I see the arc itself.
I see
The glowing thread
as it rose and peaked,
intersected with others,
lost its way. I see
The crowded pushing together
of thick weaving,
One thread so enmeshed
with others
as to be indistinguishable.

Many lost threads...
And there...
there it is emerging,
Clearer now,
on this downside of the arc,
When all that is not necessary
falls away,
And the one essence
claims its brightness
Like gold,
like the early morning sky.

*****

poems,
2020-2021

Doorway

The words of others have lost their meaning
for now - I am sitting here
with my morning tea, empty - not
waiting, just empty. A lovely
way to be on Thanksgiving Day,
having received and received
and received since birth, really-

Suddenly, the past is present
over seventy is replete with gifts:
time, releasing identity,
early memories as vivid as
a moment ago (or more so)
sight and sound as if in the next room.
Joy - sorrow - love -
moments like waves, rising and falling
the loving gift of earth being.

I act now on impulse
more than plan,
faithful to what I know is true,
has always been true.

And now we are caught
between worlds, or in worlds we knew
and now no longer know. Still,
they appear, vivid and vibrant,
sometimes more than the moment
I am living now.

And yet: here is the only reality-
the beautiful doorway
in this moment: the sweet smell
of burning wood;
the dark silence of pre-dawn;
the generous warmth given by woodfire;
the slow dawning of my Mother's being;
the tingling of my feet,
and the Presence of Light
rising within...

*****

Woodstove Teaching

This morning, I can't get the wood to catch
and stay burning: too many ashes, too little fire;
perhaps a bit like myself at this age
and in this unpredictable time - and no amount of effort-
scraping ashes, kindling, small dry wood -
none of it will carry the flame to grow.

What's more, this smoky fire covers the glass
with an orange tinge,
an accumulated smudge:
clarity is colored and lost.

Gazing at the woodstove
in this darkness just before dawn,
grateful for the outside rising temperature
giving me a break from tending
the fire in all its aspects,
I am given instead a great gift:

the woodstove in all its aspects,
its black iron presence and its warming assurance,
is a teacher: when I too accumulate too many ashes,
old repetitive thoughts, useless longings,
regrets, unrealistic wishes -
the clear glass of my soul smudges, loses
its clarity, and my inner dwelling
fills slowly with ash piles of lost moments,
unrealistic wishes, useless longings
and all the other disguises of these
sneaky visitors, persuading me otherwise.

Then the true, shining brilliant moment of now,
now alone - is lost, and I too, like the smoky glass,
like the smothering ashes - I too
have lost clarity, have lost the brilliant
shining of now in the ashes of then,
unrecoverable moments of past regrets,
and the uselessness of all
that is gone up in flames.

But now, now is always here,
her brilliance waiting gracefully
for the ashes to be shovelled out
and stored away, serving other purposes
as ashes do.
Again and again and again,
flame blown into alive presence again.

(after talking to M. yesterday.)

*****

The Poem Beneath the Poem

The poem beneath the poem
slowly emerges into words - before,
it was a negligible tide
a shifting, ever so slight,
easily ignored - but now,

now the tide has become a wave,
and the wave is rolling and growing
in size and swing -
who knows when it will become
a rogue wave? Who knows
what the tide will bring in,
flooded by its shifting waters?

We will not be ready. Every day
we will shift, even an inch, toward
the unknown. Some days it will be
several inches, or a foot, or a mile.

Who knows if we will ever reach
a steady place again?
And what does it matter?

Life will carry us...Earth will carry us,
The smallest plants and sweeps
of rain and snow will carry us, insects
and rabbits and deer and fox will carry us,
rivers and the great ancestors of trees
will carry us - and if we will not
be carried now, then we are lost.
Until Earth finds us again.

*****

Who Knows?

Who knows anything in this swirling world?
From one second to the next, the Unexpected
reigns - and though it always has -
the escalated energy of the world
lifts and twists
and pulls at the here and now
with a force unknown in our lifetime,
though not in the previous centuries
which we call History.
We are now history.

This swirling has become everyday reality.
It takes us - into the unexpected and - worse -
into the unknown.

And yet - to claim the moments of calm -
and they are there, they are many, if
we can only stay in the present moments
of our everyday world, at least a few times a day -
is to anchor the world. And not only our own world,
but the world of those around us,
and that momentary calm
weaves itself with the unfathomable numbers
doing the same in their lives, until we all
create a stream of calm light, even if
we don't know anyone else doing this...
and thus is the Light in the world
expanding over all.

"How" you might say; how?
Here is one that is given me:
Each morning, when I sit at the table with my tea
in the early morning silence, watching
the light or the breeze or stillness fill the world -
before the human race begins its escalating activity -

when I am settled,
my cat MaCushla jumps on the table,
and after sniffing the flowers
that are always at the centre
she climbs down into my lap. I have
long ago learned how to arrange my arms,
so that she settles
with her two hind paws
held by my right hand,
and her nose and front paws
snuggling into the crook of my left elbow.

Purring begins - the sound of contentment,
and then it settles too, and both of us
breathe together, sometimes
for thirty five or forty minutes
in the silence, our real garment.
I dare not move for fear she will jump down.

And this is my morning prayer,
which used to come from books, in a chapel.
Now it is the presence, the silence,
this moment only: Light,
Grace and Peace from an
intuitive cat, offering
healing rest -briefly- but daily, faithfully,
in this escalating unknown world.

*****

A Sweep of Tears

Sweeps of tears insist
on shifting open my whole body.
They soften unknown tight places
and insist on my presence
to now; now.

Rain pounding in the skylights
Dark light revealing wet morning
words shivering like tight strings
holding me together
in these
unpredictable times.

And I know, I know
with every sweep
from feet to head
and shivers spreading
in
wave
after wave

that all is happening as is
meant to happen, and that
tears are saving and softening
us all, sweeping us towards
an unforeseen relief of
finding the Great Landing Net.

*("The Great Landing Net" is an image used in the tribute to the four St. Lawrence fishermen lost to the sea in June 2020. I had taught one of them, and the father of another, when I and they were very young, fifty years ago.)

A New Ruler

Sitting at the kitchen table,
unopened books, tea cooling,
my feet begin to tingle,
spreading upward through my body,
my heart opening, spreading
into Light.

Nothing else is needed.
This moment, opening into
moment after moment after moment
is all there is.
Everything else is finished.
Everything emerging is unknown,
and more - unpredictable.

Only Now. Only Now.

The world does not revolve around me,
a bare fact I cannot seem to truly believe.
Expectation rules me. It is time
to find a new ruler. I must learn
to lose...or better - give everything away-
watching the light arrive -
enough, enough.

*****

No Comfortable Bench

Life is no comfortable bench
it is hard and slippery
requiring body adjustments
constantly -
a straight back, an attentive
posture, a keen seeing-
outwardly, yes, but -
especially as time unfolds -
an inward focus
sharpens the gaze
as the forward path
of the heart's direction
appears like sunrise.

It is only then that the path forward
really begins. It is only then
that layers of possibilities appear,
often hiding the heart's light.
It is only then that
the comfortable bench appears
less and less often,
and instead - the certain glow
of an occasional, growing light.

*****

Falling Away

All those years of my life
given over to "techniques" for silence,
for contemplative presence,
for breathing practices...on and on...
all falling away like eye shades
put on for protection
and taken off for clearer seeing -
all falling away-
almost like a walker someone uses
to help them walk, and then -
it's no longer needed.

I am stepping into what is —
only what is
glowing and tingling in the moment -
and in moment after moment after moment -
and what is, focused on - present to -
lights up, even on a dark day-
ah! Sacred.

*****

The Magnificent Whole

For that split second only - looking
at the trees outside the screened porch
from my early morning place
at the kitchen table -

the raindrops on one leaf sparkled -
sparkled! in all possible colours
and in a few seconds, went back
to being indistinguishable raindrops
on a branch's edge.

Isn't that the way we all - everything
in creation - all of us - live in this world?
We sparkle a awhile, perhaps
even a few times - and then we are
restored to our natural inclusion
with the myriad rest of creation,
blessedly indistinguishable
from the unfathomable glory
of the Magnificent Whole.

*****

Only Now, Only Here

The air itself - certainly the air of my life -
is changing day by day.
Heart is vibrating as I write this:
heat, rhythm, expanding -
Presence, presence...only now
only here.
Silence and settling, but
only in the unfolding
moment by moment.
Today the trees are still,
sky is grey, expectant -
Rain. Rain.

*****

Stream of Grace

Rain, pouring and pelting
keeps us in, containing us,
delaying the usual morning walk
offering us instead this delicious - yes-
delicious silence. Only the rain,
that soft gift, van be heard.
Now and then a bird song,
as they shelter in the trees.

This is my morning heaven.
This is my stream of grace.
This is the day's beginning
the world remaking itself
after resting in fertile darkness,
steeped in silence.

And isn't that how we too
are remade?
Steeping in the fertile silence
of sleep, and the silence
of the dark and fertile emptiness
of the world?

*****

Freed

Lee loved life: she followed
the flow of it. She would not
be pinned down in any way -
and this brought her as much
sorrow as joy.

Thus she changed from lab work
to Real Estate: freed to wander
all over the county and the world:
freed.

Whatever enclosed her she
stepped over, went beyond -
knowing nothing of why,
or caring about it either. Other
countries intrigued her-
travel compelled her -
and always more and beyond.

Her inner push also freed
impatience and inconsistent
unpredictable behaviour,
puzzling and hurting for those
who loved her - for she drew
love as much as distress.
Lee lived both and brought forth both
into the worlds of those who loved her.

Finally, she blossomed. Truth
rose in her like a fountain:
she knew. She knew without doubt
when it was time for her

to leave this world - that most
inescapable of mandates.
She announced it,
prepared as much as she could
and left us all - as puzzling
in death as she so often was in life-
but so free in those last days
that a Light shone from her certainty
her grace, her freedom.

And her reconciliations with those
she had hurt most.

And now we look out for owls-
for in her certain freedom
she announced her return as one
of that most mysterious of birds.

Lee has not left us.
She has merely changed her form
and waits, waits for her loved ones
in ways and places and shapes
she could never carry out
in her earth-life.

(written at the request of Mary Keats, Lee Gauthier's friend)

Arrival: Pandemic Poem

The rising of tears within, sweeping
from feet to chest to eyes
signals fatigue, I am told -
but it is more than that.

It is the grief of unknown endings
foretelling a falling away
of what was firm and unquestioned.
Even now, it is not negotiable,
just a reality arriving, not invited,
not chosen.

And announcing the arrival
of a Greater Presence than
what was previously known,
a burgeoning Unknown, both
softening and loving,
dark and unyielding
in its inescapable reality
and its gentle tender arrival.

*****

Only Here

It is only here - this solitude,
this empty heart - everyone else
gathered around but not in
my innerheart - that I know
who I am. Finally, if briefly.

And that those to whom I feel closest
are inside my inmost heart:
they do not feel tears rush through my body;
they do not feel my darkness;
empty of everything, however brief;
they do not feel the silence filling me;
they do not notice the forgotten flower,
half hidden in a ditch, waving;
they do not see the worms in the road,
or the frog crushed by a passing car;
(and if they did they would probably not remove them)
they do not feel that rush of blood, that helplessness -

I could go on. But why? Everyone,
Everyone feels her own heart alone,
and it is only Love, and Love alone,
in all its winding forms
that opens any Heart, and only for a breath -
any longer would be unbearable -

to see and hold and be the world!

*****

A Shiver of Tears

The world is watered by tears.
I can only believe
that they make things grow -
dissolve the old, soften
hard ground, water inner seeds,
call forth new life where death
appears to be the ruler.

Every day more tears appear,
especially if one watches
the daily news of wars, deaths,
floods, murders, and all the ways
humans dissolve the world-
bringing tears - to soften,
to dissolve.

Is it tears then, that water the world
into life? Are tears the great dissolvers,
the powerful softeners for what is next
meant to emerge?

As my own body feels
a shiver of tears running
through it almost every day,
feels the softening they bring,
the readying for new light,
the dissolving of tight darkness-

Let it be so. Let it be so.

The Magnificent Whole

For that split second only - looking
at the trees outside the screened porch
from my early morning place at the kitchen table-
the raindrops on them sparkled -
sparkled! in all possible colours -
and in a few seconds, went back
to being indistinguishable raindrops
on a leaf's dripping edge.
Isn't this the way we all - everything
created -(which is everything) -
live in this world?
We sparkle awhile, perhaps even
a few times - and then we are
restored to our natural inclusion
with the whole of created life,
blessedly indistinguishable
from the unfathomable glory
of the magnificent Whole.

*****

Part II

A SEVERER LISTENING:
(a la Adrienne Rich)

1. Poems from self, poems to self

stream after stream dries up
and falls away, streams where I spent my life,
searching
diving
looking
reaching for…

a new and unfamiliar warmth
inhabits my heart, briefly.
It happens
at the sight of wounded animals
and birds, insects and flowers.
It happens
at my utter helplessness
to make anyone's life better –

it happens
as I wipe the counter
feed the cat
respond to emails
make the bed
weed the garden

And then it disappears.

2.

Someone is digging shovelfuls
of old dirt
from deep inside my heart. A grave –
but who or what will be buried there?
Or no one will,
or nothing. Perhaps
I will live with an empty grave
in my heart
for the rest of my earthly life, and –
after that –
who knows? who
knows?

And perhaps I am just one small
insignificant grave
as the grave of the whole world
is being dug.

Watch the evening news.

3.

All the dark waves of old pain
have rolled themselves into one
and are towering towards me,
a tidal wave
of immeasurable proportions.

Is this what is called "a rogue wave?"
unexpected,
an overpowering surprise
of deathly proportions?

I breathe.
I allow it to roll over me,
through me.
I surrender, finally,
to the whole of my life,
and my death, when it
opens its arms.

4.

The wave has subsided,
though I nearly
drowned in it yesterday,
I nearly started the next personal war,
nearly shot projectiles of rage,
anger, blame, explosions of grief
into the air around me, no
matter who was hurt – I
came to the edge –
and held them. Held her-
that tiny, beaten lost child
never seen, never truly loved.
I tried to release her,
time after time
but she clung and clung,
not wanting to go,
unable to bear
yet another rejection.

But this morning the wave
has receded and I am
present again, grown up, seeing
her, holding her,
reassuring her –

that when the wave returns
as waves must and will –
she is safe in my arms,
and I in hers.

5.

I am back to praying, loudly in my heart,
as I did in childhood.
I am back to fingering beads,
the last resort of mystery
of pleading, of helplessness.

I am back inside the realm of Soul
realizing for the first time
that I was never out of it
but only in a cocoon of arrogance
living in small mind
keeping heart carefully hidden
in a fancy box,
taking it out only when it suited me.

All that is gone now, though
I suspect it will continue
to pound and pound
on my door for a very long time,
perhaps forever, perhaps
to the moment when it
stops, realizing
there will be no answer.
No answer.

The beads will bring me
back to reality
every time I am tempted.

6. No More Room

There has arisen in me a hunger
a starvation, really, for great spaciousness.
There is no more room – for how long,
I'd like to know, but can't –
for words upon words, for book after book,
for mountains of sentences
lying before me.

There is no more room for beautiful websites,
full of astounding teachings,
words
of deep blessing and encouragement
and ways to enter spiritual mysteries.
They are superfluous now.
I send them to spam.

There is no more room inside me.
I am full. There is only now
opening to the fullness of no words,
opening to a Presence not captured
by any words at all. All words
make it small. All words fall
far short of its Reality – and –
not only fall far short – but
try to fit the Presence into
another's understanding,
describable, comprehensible.
Which it isn't.

There is no description. There is no understanding.
And there is No More Room for Words,
hoping for either, looking for both.

What there is – is
Being. Light. Darkness. Elusive Presence.
And for a few moments,
a few moments at a time (any more is
unbearable, intolerable) there is
a Weight of Being tenderly approaching,
careful of capacity, standing just there,
just there,
next to my small, confused,
frightened and fearful heart.

7.

Peeling itself back, the birch bark
wrapping the tall, thick trees
outside my window
is undoing me
once again.

I never see it except my heart
lurches with connection;
I feel my own heart peeling
and peeling, freeing the huge flame
that hasn't gone out all these years.

Might it consume me?

It would not be a terrible way
to leave the world.

8. The Cave of Despair

I must claim my despair now
as the true companion that she is.
I cannot deny her any longer.
She has been with me as long as memory,
though I have castigated, beaten,
denied, ignored and run from her.

Here she is now, more alive than ever,
claiming me. There is nothing more
I can do to avoid her. No good thought
or self-loving practice
will dispel her.
Instead
I must love her. She has waited for me,
patiently, all my life.
I see now that she came into
the world with me,
lived with me
in my mother's womb
before I was born.
She grew with me –
but I always found a way to deny her
hide her like a shameful
deformed family member in olden times.

But here she is. My bare truth,
and at this late age
I turn and see her. She is painfully difficult
to behold – I want to cover my eyes
and turn away –
I have denied her all my life –
but she is me. She is me.

Dark, misshapen,
crippled, blind – wrapped
in black dissolving rags, crawling
on hands and knees – I must go to her,
sit with her, hold and rock her
in our mutual tears and ask her
ask her now,
to lead me back into light
(if I was ever really there)

Time to live in the cave of despair
for awhile.

9. Shaft of Light

Nothing is every completely true
as it is spoken.
What I want to say to you is shadowed and shaped
by all that went before
in each of our lives
and by whatever is swirling within us
around us,
when we speak.
What I perceive, and even more –
what I understand –
is the smallest of parts
surrounded by all unknown.

There is no single truth
about anyone, anything.
There is only what I perceive
to be true, a small thread of light
running through all things
changing second by millisecond.
And it is in this shifting universe
that you/I/we
try to see one another
relate to one another
speak truth to one another
love, one another. Amazing
it happens at all.

10. The True World

The true world is not the one out there – not
the one I am looking at in all its
needs and demands and schedules
and expectations and must haves –
though

the true world can be glimpsed,
glimpsed only – not captured -
in light on leaves,
on the dark floor of the forest
in the thick silence or the sudden wind –
in the surprise gift
of a caterpillar weaving, weaving
(o miracle of miracles)
the cocoon that will take his form
completely, so that
he will not recognize himself at all.

Through all these and a million other lenses
the true world mirrors
the inner heart of a person, or perhaps
it's the other way around.
Or both at once.

A bridge of light links those worlds:
the true world within
the true world without.

11. Nothing is My Name

In many ways I am still
trying to be the good girl
The one who meets and surpasses all expectations.

I am trying to be a good
Friend
Niece/aunt
Partner/companion
Sister of Mercy -

But I am tired, so tired of all the roles
That saved me, all my life,
All my life.

But - without them -
I am no one I can name. No one
I can see. Nothing
Is my name
(As it soon will anyway be)

I am leaving the world of advice
Practices, new ways
Of finding peace and
Positive self-images, self
Being the focus word.

So far I am finding nothing
to replace them.
Nothing -

Turning into sadness, loss,
Deep aloneness - and
Back to nothing
In its turn.

I look down at myself:
Is this the body
That houses Nothing?
It seems so -

I try to believe Rumi, who says
"The crowd of sorrows" may just be clearing us out
For some new delight," but I cannot, cannot
Know that yet.

My Guest House is entirely empty.
Entirely.

12. Slow Grace

I thought I would know more,
Understand more, be more certain
As I got older - but the opposite -
Dear God -
The opposite is true -

I know less
I understand less
I am less certain

Of anything

But a new Presence rises
Like a sun or a full moon
Within me - a Presence
Needing no knowing or understanding
And - least of all - any certainty -

The slow grace of letting go
Of everything
Has begun

13. Before Dawn: the One is the All

Sitting at the table before dawn, I was swept away, so it seemed, by a sense that the One is the All.; it is this concrete reality that allows me to focus on one tree, one flower or leaf, and feel the heartbeat of the whole Cosmos vibrating in my heart and heating my whole body. My little gardens can be small - are getting smaller every year - but one flower, one blade of grass, opens the entire cosmos in my being.

14. Disguises

Old veils are burning, burning away
from what they have been concealing…

What I thought was truth in time
only clothes a glowing energy
of being, of presence and
all the outer garments are now
in tatters, dissolving
in age and grace.

The veils were necessary disguises
for that bright essence, hiding it
from people I disliked or feared,
or thought strange and closed.
They protected the tender wounds
of pain, of hurt and loss, of misunderstanding
and excruciating self-doubt.

But now the veils are smoldering,
leaving holes the size of countries
or stars, revealing lights the size
of planets in every soul I know.

Age purifies the soul of all,
all its necessary disguises.

16. Dissolving

Really, when you think about it, when you
look back through all known history -
(and then consider the unknown history too);
when you step inwardly
aside and view your own small life
in all its glories and achievements and
hidden failures and pretentious pride;

when you have lived enough to realize
that no other kind of life is possible
for anyone, no matter your position,
your education, your riches or your poverty,
when you are so desperate that you can
surrender all you ever had or knew
(or thought you had, or thought you knew);

then you can dissolve. You can
open your arms and your heart
and release everything, everyone
whom you ever loved, or ever thought you hated
(and really - is there any such thing - hatred
being only the caged-in wires of fear, irritation,
short-sightedness and small thinking -

hidden in them all is the thread of light
that lives in every created thing, from caterpillar
to mouse to hawk to tree to water -
and sometimes (but not always, not always)
in human beings
you get the drift -
stars shine overhead every night to remind us,
even in the dark -

but seeing becomes better after all righteousness,
achievement, judgment, projections, fear
impatience, greed, and just plain crankiness
fall into the black hole of dissolving...

Then Light begins to show herself more frequently,
becomes an easy-going, undemanding companion,
a teacher of letting go, letting be,
opening doors and levelling stairs so
walking through this lifetime
brings more and more of Herself
into the dark Realms
that threaten the world.

17. Illumination

Now I glimpse the world
within the world. The world
that is the world.
I move my head and a shaft of light
appears. I move it back
and the shaft is gone.

Leaves open their
delicate skins to reveal light
not there a second ago.

The sun is revelation,
appearing and disappearing,
diving into water's depths
and peeling bark of birch
all at once.

I don't know where to look.
I don't know how to take in
the presences all around me –
but –revelation – neither do I have to –

I only have to see what is there.
And bow in silence.
And bow in silence.

Illumination is not knowing.

(for Contemplative Photography Class
/MikSang Practice,
Fleming College, July 2018
Brenda Peddigrew)

Conclusion: Word Paintings

*But here it is – I have lived through words
too long to abandon them completely, even
when I recognize their limits.
Instead, I let them propel me
beyond even their own limits!
Instead, I let them shoot me
out of their cannons!*

And then I paint their wordless meanings.

www.ingramcontent.com/pod-product-compliance
Lightning Source LLC
Chambersburg PA
CBHW030904080526
44589CB00010B/139